MW00627772

Past Medical History

Recollections of a Medical Miscreant

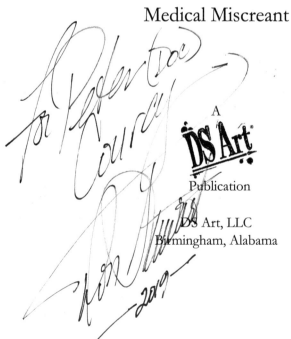

A

DS Art.

Publication

DS Art, LLC
Birmingham, Alabama

DS Art, LLC
2805 Crescent Avenue
Birmingham. AL 35209

Portions of several chapters have appeared previously
in print and online, in the Birmingham Arts Journal,
The Dead Mule School of Southern Literature, Pulse magazine,
Southern Humorists, and as blog posts at
www.DSArt.com

For generous permission to quote from his work,
the author wishes to thank Steven Pressfield,
The Warrior Ethos, © 2011 Black Irish Books

First DS Art Paperback Edition August 2013

ISBN: 0-9773294-2-7

Printed in the United States of America

Past Medical History

A narrative or record of past events
and circumstances that are or may be relevant
to a patient's current state of health.

For J.L.

The hardest thing in the world is to be ourselves.

Who are we? Our family tells us, society tells us, laws
and customs tell us. But what do *we* say?
How do we get to that place of self-knowledge
and conviction where we are able to state
without doubt, fear or anger,
"This is who I am, this is what I believe,
this is how I intend to live my life."

- Steven Pressfield
The Warrior Ethos

Life is like a really easy video game.
But you've only got one guy.

- Robben Leaf

Preface

It took me nearly thirty years to write this book.

I've been telling some of these stories for longer than that, and began trying to commit them to paper as soon as writing stopped being an academic obligation. The advent of word processors and personal computers made that job easier, allowing me to file my memories away in neatly labeled virtual documents, conveniently categorized in iconic virtual folders.

I write in the winter, in January and February, after the seasonal rush of holiday gift sales, the busiest time of the year for a retail artist, and before the onset of the spring craft show season. The studio is quiet. The phone seldom rings. I have the time then to sift through an accumulation of handwritten notes recorded days, weeks and miles apart in show booths and hotel rooms, between sales pitches, picture sketches, take-out dinners and late night movies on someone else's cable TV.

In February of this year I was talking to an acquaintance in the publishing business, and mentioned that some day I might like to see if my stories were print-worthy. Some day when I had more experience, of course, and enough material to actually fill a book. "How many stories have you got?" he wanted to know. A quick click on the folder marked "Past Medical History" told me there were over a hundred.

Hoping to knit them all into one cohesive narrative, I arranged the pieces in chronological order, threw half of them away, and suddenly found that the remaining stories formed the arc of a tale on their own – and revealed for the first time not only why I felt compelled to leave medicine behind (the reasons for that were apparent at the time), but also why I chose to pursue art as a second career. It was an odd choice then, and remains so in retrospect; something chosen (I always thought) as a matter of convenient coincidence rather than a part of my persona that reaches as far back, and springs from the same deep root as my interest in medical science.

Perhaps *Past Medical History* is not so much a story of a doctor who lost his way, as it is the tale of an artist who stayed in the hospital just long enough to get over his distractions.

Don Stewart, Artist
August 2013

Curriculum

Graduation

Internship

Commencement

Appendix

Acknowledgements

Past Medical History

Introduction

Past Medical History

The man had nine tubes connected to his body on the day he died.

Two IVs directed fluids and medications, drugs flowing into one arm to keep his blood pressure up, in the other to coax the pressure back down, with antibiotics, anti-emetics, acid blockers, blood thinners and pain killers piggy-backed onto Y-shaped access ports, or pumped in measured doses through blue computerized boxes clamped to shiny metal IV poles.

A third line penetrated deep into the man's chest, entering above his collar bone, coursing through the great thoracic vessels and the right-side chambers of his heart, its round balloon tip resting snugly in the terminal arteries of his lungs. Above, a thin yellow feeding tube emerged spaghetti-like from his nose, while down below a thick red rubber catheter drained the man's bladder into a bag hooked onto the side of his bed. Another did what it could to channel the volumes of liquid feces that had plagued this patient for too many days, and took up far too much of the intensive care nurses' valuable time in sanitary maintenance, skin care and linen changes.

Clear plastic tubes the size of small garden hoses exited either side of the patient's chest, each connected to a low-suction vacuum canister that functioned to keep his fragile lungs inflated – lungs that had already popped like loose bubble-wrap from the air forced into them through a similar tube that traversed the length of his throat. This was the tube he had hoped to avoid. The one that just one week earlier he had made me promise, *promise* not to let anyone put into him.

Cut Out

On June 30th, 1986, my medical degree was a year old. I had just completed an internship in surgery, managed to pass the third and final round of my general medical board exams, and had been issued a license to practice medicine in a large Midwestern state. At the stroke of five p.m. that day I was also gleefully unemployed, and exited the hospital in the middle of afternoon rounds, feeling like I had just been released from prison.

I did not plan to return.

With four more years of training required to finish my surgical residency, this behavior represented an abrupt and unanticipated deviation from procedure within the structured world of academic medicine. It also ended my lifelong plan to be a doctor.

It has been said – on reputable authority, I might add, by extremely important people who are highly regarded and widely published in the medical literature – that I *washed out* of the medical profession. Petered out. Rose to my level of professional incompetence, then burned out, bailed out, dropped out. That I just wasn't cut out for the job.

Could be. I most certainly *walked* out. Or, as I like to say, *fled* – in a quiet, dignified manner, characteristic of the noble calling of surgeons. And on my own terms, at that.

Those who had seen this happen before (rarely, mind you - many may become disillusioned with the call, but few actually abandon this, the most sacred of learned professions) said with an awe-ful and profound certainty that I would surely be back, and sooner rather than later. You could count on that.

The house bet was that I would last a year, maybe, though some only gave me six months at the most. Just long enough to get a real taste of life on the outside, stripped of all the comfort and respect and social insulation imparted by the Aesculapian mantle. After all, you don't train this long just to throw it all away. No one does.

Oh, yes, they said. He'll be back. Just as soon as he gets his head straight.

Lucky for me, that never happened.

Past Medical History

My career in medicine began when I was three years old.

Holding tightly to my father's hand at the end of a dark hospital corridor, I was unable to keep up with the heavy, sibilant stream of conversation flowing between Daddy and Dr. Mashburn, the man who had delivered me, who had sewn up my chin after a slip in the bathtub a month before, who was explaining now the details of Mommy's condition.

My attention was drawn away from the confusing drone of grown-up words to a bright black and white picture shining down from a lighted box on the wall. The "x-array" film clearly demonstrated a gleaming white shaft of bone (my mother's clavicle – a word unknown to me at the time) with a perfectly round, black spot in the middle. One day I would understand this spot to be a hole in my mother's skeleton, a spherical defect caused by the benign overgrowth of a certain type of white blood cell. Such x-ray findings were evidence of an *eosinophilic granuloma*, the source of my mother's pain.

I knew then that children weren't supposed to interrupt their parents, especially when they were talking to someone as important as the doctor. I also knew, even at that age, that there weren't supposed to be dark round holes in people's bodies. Tapping into my preschool fund of medical knowledge, I generated my first working differential diagnosis, eliminated the least likely possibilities, and tugged on my father's hand to offer my conclusion. Pointing up to the radiograph, I posited my first clinical hypothesis:

"Is that Mommy's belly button?"

***

The doctors blasted my mother's disease with high doses of radiation, the technological hammer that for half a century conveniently turned every conceivable medical malady into a nail. As expected, the globules of cells that were eroding her skeleton simply melted away, and for a time she was free of pain.

After a short while, though, the ache in her bones returned, and would stay with her for the days she had remaining. No benign tumors this time. In less than a year a cancer that had been hiding deep inside her invaded her abdomen and her thin skeletal frame, consuming her body as readily as the radiation once liquefied her granulomas.

We never knew where her cancer came from, this insidious disease that abbreviated her thirtieth year, and claimed her just a week before my fifth birthday. My father believed that it was a result of the radiation treatments. When I was grown, Dr. Mashburn told me that to his recollection it was a straightforward bone cancer. Laboratory tests indicated an origin in the thyroid, while the pattern of abdominal spread strongly suggested ovarian disease. Unfortunately, none of these malignancies mirrored my mother's clinical course, and none offered any hope of effective treatment. Given the rudimentary understanding of cancer in the early 1960's, it is almost certain that we will never know for sure what killed her. What we do know is that she was taken from us very quickly.

I Like My Job

"*I like my job*," my friend Cam used to say, filling in the minute
or so it took to tune his guitar strings between songs. "I get up
early, around *ten a.m*…" (brief pause for a skitter of laughter) "…
shuffle to the kitchen and pick at a tune or two, while I wait for
the java to brew. *Then* I take a coffee break. It's a tough life…
but so far I've been able to handle it pretty well."

Poet, singer, songwriter, luthier, steadily booked performer – Cam
was no slouch. Back in college, he had turned down a full ride on
an engineering scholarship, switching mid-term of his freshman
year to major instead in graphic design.

"You know, the *creative thing,*" he explained to me once.

Around the same time he also picked up a guitar, and found another outlet for his restless ingenuity.

"…After breakfast (a meal known to most people as… *lunch*…),
I write songs for an hour or two … before stretching out for a
well-deserved *nap*." He offers his audience a well-rehearsed, conspiratorial grin. "I might make a few phone calls in the afternoon,
then walk downtown to the coffee shop. Maybe I'll grab a pen
and write a few more lines, or hang out with friends, or just wait
for my Muse to arrive and inspire me… Then I come back home
and tune my guitar, and pretty soon the Muse and me, well, we'll
come up with something a little bit like *this*."

I asked him how an engineer-in-training, how someone so familiar with left-brain order could transition completely to an artistic
lifestyle. Where did all the math go?

"It's in the *chords*, man," he said to me patiently, emphatically, speaking as though he had been asked to explain sunshine to a child. "The math is in the music, dude."

Then he laughed, a half-chuckled *huh*, little more than a cough with a grin. "Can you see me with a short haircut and a pocket protector? *That* would be wacky, man."

He kept the numbers in his head, but somehow they made their way to his fingers, the long way - through the bruises of his heart.

Most weekends, Cam would pack up his guitar and sound system, and spend three to five hours a night performing for live audiences in taverns, coffee houses, theatres and music halls across the Midwest. Audiences sang along, groupies bought him dinner and coffee, new fans took home copies of his latest self-published CD. Local musicians would gather after the show, and jam with him until three in the morning.

"I get up early, around *ten a.m.*..."

Cam discovered his mother's body hanging from the ceiling when he was six years old. Both of his parents were alcoholic. His dad abandoned the family long before the day my friend walked home from school, a first grader, to learn the most indelible lesson of his life.

Cam spent every one of the years I knew him fighting anger, depression, alcohol and drugs. He beat his exogenous addictions using his colossal brainpower, deciding from one day to the next as an intellectual exercise to stop drinking, stop smoking dope. He even beat tobacco. The internal demons he exorcised through his music.

"I guess there are better jobs out there, but I haven't found one yet," he liked to say.

He used his songs to heal others, too, reaching out to people in nursing homes and halfway houses, working and performing in prisons and elementary schools. Not surprisingly, he held a special fondness for kids in the primary grades. "Gotta wake 'em up early," he used to say, "Before life gets a chance to kick 'em in the guts."

It seems trite to say that Cam was an inspiration, but that's just precisely what he was, even after the fact. "Sure, you can stay in the System, try and change things from the inside. But how much of you is gonna die in the process? You need your whole self involved, man, if you're gonna do something as hard as telling the truth."

Cam was a man of his words. You know, the *creative thing*.

I guess there are better jobs out there, but I haven't found one yet.

Pre Pre-Med

Highlights

Over the course of my mother's tragic illness, she made count-
less trips to the doctor's office and the hospital for examinations,
tests, procedures, treatments, delayed recoveries. Often as not, my
brother and I were carried along, left to spend the hours by ourselves in hospital waiting rooms, where we were supposed to *be
quiet* while the grown-ups consulted with doctors and nurses, or
'visited' down the corridor beyond the closed double doors with
the circular windows, where they whispered together in some
faraway room where children were forbidden to appear.

My brother, a first-grader, could read a little bit, which meant that
we were usually left in the care of Dr. Seuss and his colorful staff
of whimsical babysitters. Both of us pointed to the pictures while
brother read aloud, and I memorized the rhymes, thinking all the
while that I was reading, too. He did the same with dog-eared
stacks of *Highlights* magazines, the only juvenile literature available
in waiting rooms in those days, save for the occasional Golden
Book, or *The Children's Bible*, which in spite of its florid illumina-
tion was far out of reach for the beginning reader. Whether or
not he could accurately translate the captions, my brother ably
narrated the comic adventures of Tommy Timbertoes in *Highlights*, as well as the handful of illustrated stories that filled the
magazine's pages, and thereby occupied many of our idle hours.

It was he who introduced me to the most enchanting part of
Highlights: the Hidden Pictures. For kids of every age, everywhere,
this regular feature defined the allure of the magazine, and kept
us endlessly entertained and usually out of trouble.

The magic of the Hidden Pictures page cannot be overstated.

Each black and white line drawing depicted a deceptively simple scene: a bedroom, a kitchen, a backyard swing. Yet cleverly concealed among the lines of the curtains, the wallpaper, the tree bark, leaves and grass were outlines of everyday items: a toothbrush, a funnel, a comb. The reader's task was to identify each of a dozen items listed on the facing page, and hidden somewhere within the picture. Courteous kids who had already searched the page would locate the hidden images, and check off the ones they had found on the adjacent list. Others would circle the items with a pencil – or worse, a pen – spoiling the fun for the rest of us.

But only some of the fun. For me, the fascination of the Hidden Pictures transcended the challenge of the puzzle. At such an early age, I was utterly amazed by the drawings themselves – and the fact that someone, somewhere, not only was able to *draw a picture* (a magical feat in itself), but somehow miraculously included things that could not possibly occur in real life. Who could imagine a frying pan hiding in a goldfish bowl? Scissors in a pair of suspenders? A slice of apple pie in a wagon wheel? Amazing! In a time and place where strict rules governed every aspect of children's behavior, the *Highlights* Hidden Pictures page was a glorious expression of visual anarchy.

Looking back, the Hidden Pictures feature was perhaps the only place where children were allowed – *encouraged* in fact – to think and smile at the same time. Sesame Street had yet to make its television debut. The whole concept of edutainment lay a decade in the future. Aside from children's books and comics (where we were required to learn the illustrated stories without variation), or coloring books (which quite literally discouraged thinking outside of the lines), the Hidden Pictures permitted us a rare opportunity to exercise our young detective brains, come up with our own narratives for a scene, and then, if we were so inclined, try and explain the unlikely presence of these extraneous objects, the ones that clearly didn't belong, yet were added specifically for our enjoyment by someone whose intelligence and artistic ability appeared to border on the supernatural.

The pages of *Highlights* magazine impressed and influenced me at a profound level, instilling a love for quirky imagery that lay dormant in my brain until it could be awakened years later, when I was a student in college. In an odd way, this was a gift from my mother, a creative time capsule that waited for just the right moment to spring open, and alter the course of my life.

Bob War

Hung up like a frozen bug on a spider web, my tiny body bobbed rhythmically a foot above the ground, front-back, up-down, front-back, in a slowly dying circular motion. Mouth open wide, I attempted to cry out, but the fear was overwhelming, wider and deeper than the pain. I was afraid to move, even to breathe. Spit pooled beneath my tongue, spilled down my chin with a silent flow of tears, and spattered into the dust where it mingled with fresh crimson pearls of blood that dripped from tiny cuts in the tented skin of my arms and legs.

We were out together on a fishing trip, not long after my mother's funeral: dad, granddad, brother, and me. Just off for the afternoon; it would do everyone good. Grandpa hauled a borrowed aluminum boat in the back of his rusted red pickup and drove us all to a neighbor's farm, bouncing along the way to the pond at the far end of the middle forty. We followed a parallel track of bare dirt cut through acres of cattle pasture, bordered on all sides by ancient brown barbed wire strung between ranks of weathered grey railroad ties and chest-high cedar stumps. Grandpa stopped the truck at the corner of the field and got out, lifting the loop of wire that held the hand-made gate, nothing but three or four rows of "bob-war" stapled to a few sturdy branches and strung across the gap. Lift the loop, drive through, stop, get out, stretch the gate back across the road, loop it shut again.

The dusty dirt track followed the fence line for a couple dozen yards before it split to circumnavigate an oasis of willow and cottonwood trees, ringed around a small body of water. This was a naturally occurring pond (differentiated in these parts from a *tank*, a pool of artificial construction, created by a bulldozer operator over the course of a weekend) an acre or two in size, with an irregular border of grass and weeds, and a scattering of lily pads and cattails that promised a bounty of fish. We were told that this spot had not been exploited by anglers for a while, not since the owner's kids had grown and gone off to college, and since it was likely to be a while longer before they brought any grandkids of their own to bother the fish, we might as well avail ourselves of the opportunity.

The track that bent back around the pond and into itself was joined in one place by a side trail, more a path for the cattle than an actual road, but wide enough to accommodate a pickup truck or tractor when needed. A new set of corner posts had recently been sunk on the spot, and a new suspension gate constructed using heavy galvanized wire that still retained its dull silver hue.

My brother and I took turns pairing with the grown-ups, one group at a time in the boat, the other pair taking positions around the pond, wherever the weeds gave access to the water, and the ground was flat enough to set up a folding chair. According to the habits and disposition of a physically healthy five-year-old, I danced freely about the perimeter of the pond, plopping hook and bobber into the water here and there, whenever there wasn't anything more interesting to occupy my fancy, like chasing dragonflies or pointing a finger too closely at the green, greasy, irregular layers of a fresh cow patty, squealing "EEEeewwww!" loud enough to chase away the green bottle flies and distract everyone else from the lazy business at hand. Not surprisingly, my approach to angling yielded little in the way of positive results.

After some while my grandfather invited me to come with him into the boat, and for an hour or so we tossed worms, crickets, and minnows over the side in a generous act of feeding only slightly larger baitfish. Now and again a bobber would dip, and we might pull up a hand-sized bluegill (my hand, not granddad's), but the promise of the farmer's aquatic bounty was never fully realized.

Only once did my oversized red and white float plunge below the surface of the water, and that happened while I was busy investigating the contents of the tackle box, asking grandpa if he didn't have some cookies or crackers or something else I could eat to take my mind off the fact that we weren't catching anything. "Ho!" he cried, and grabbed for my fishing rod, just before it lurched over the side of the boat. "That's gotta be a big one!" he said, but before he could reach the reel and set the hook, the bobber popped up a good ten feet from where it went under, and quietly resumed the passive activity for which it was named.

Disappointed when the line came back empty, and with a clean hook besides, I fussed and whined as indulged children can, until Grandpa decided that it was as good a time as any to beach the boat and take on a new crew.

For me, it was a good time to stretch my legs. I remember running around in circles in the pasture, catching yellow sulfur butterflies and chasing winged grasshoppers until the sun began to set. The meadowlarks chirred and whistled from the fence posts, the blackbirds flocked to the pond with their chattering racket, and I ran around and around with arms outstretched, buzzing like an airplane motor. I heard the truck start up as Daddy and Grandpa pulled the boat from the water, and prepared to head back home. They called my name, and I ran toward their voices, rounding the long curve of the dusty road with a smile on my face and the warmth of baby fat burning through my tiny legs, oscillating pistons that carried me swiftly down the path. "Hurry up!" they called. "Hurry up! It's time to go!"

And I did hurry, afraid in the way of five-year-olds that I might be forgotten and left behind. *Hurry* was the word that filled my mind as I strove to lengthen my stride, pointing my legs and feet forward in a straight line, propelling myself into the air between bouncing steps.

It's not as though I never knew what hit me. I knew exactly what had happened the moment it occurred, which unfortunately turned out to be one moment too late. The leaden strands of new, off-the-coil barbed wire that stretched across the shadowed path had caught me mid-stride and held me there like Velcro, just high enough so that my sneakered toes were unable to make contact with the ground. The recoil of the wire juddered me to the bones, but instead of slinging me backward onto the ground, the vibrations served only to wedge the twisted metal barbs deeper into my tender skin as I trembled in vertical orbit, unable to move otherwise, too hurt and too terrified to do anything of my own volition.

Daddy was the first on the scene. It took only seconds for him to realize that his noisy son had gone suddenly mute, and that only something serious could account for that. He carefully lifted me from the sharpened points, one prong, one limb at a time, allowing each taught wire to hum back into line, the deepest string on a bass guitar.

He carried me back to the tailgate of the pick up truck, to be consoled and evaluated. From somewhere, Grandma's cookies appeared, and soon the world became a warmer, softer place.

The marks on my forehead and biceps and the back of my hand have long since faded away, but I still have scars on my leg, two small white ovals, perfectly arranged in the middle of my thigh, another on the ridge of my shin. People seldom got stitches in those days, even for full-thickness penetration wounds that gaped white-rimmed and open-mouthed beneath the sick pinky-brown cover of self-stick bandages. Paint on the Mercurochrome, put on a Band-Aid. Stop complaining. Sure it hurts, but you'll live, won't you? You should have watched where you were going, anyway.

Had I known, I would have. After that experience, you bet I did.

Later on I would be reminded of that afternoon, whenever I pushed the curved points of fishing hooks through the soft pads of patients' palms and fingertips, clipping the barbs with wire cutters before slipping the headless hooks backwards, and down, and out. This was a trick I learned not from the lecture hall or any medical text, but from books on camping and woodcraft, read on hot summer days beside grass-rimmed ponds in the middle of cattle fields.

First Grade, First Day

Following Mrs. Brown's instructions, we reached into our school bags and got out our new Big Chief blue-lined manila paper tablets, along with our giant first grade pencils - the fat ones intended to fit snugly into clumsy first grade fists - each fitted with a bubble-gum pink eraser the size of a gumdrop, anticipating an abundance of first grade mistakes. These we placed in front of us, the pencils laid to rest in smooth grooves cut neatly into the tops of our desks. We would need them later, Mrs. Brown said. For now, we would use our *colors*, big cigar-sized crayons in the standard eight-pack of primary and secondary hues, plus brown and black. Take out the red one, and do as I do.

Open your tablets, she said, her taught straight back turned to us, her hand raised to the blackboard, her voice as crisp as her starched plaid cotton dress. We were going to learn to write today. We were going to learn to *pay attention.* I did so, or tried to, distracted as I was by the stunning display unfolding before me.

Mrs. Brown was writing in *red.* And she wasn't writing words, either. I knew that much right away. She was drawing a picture. In *colored* chalk!

Crayons I understood. Chalk, too. We'd seen it in kindergarten, and at home in the sewing room. Sometimes Grandma let us use it to make hop-scotch squares on the sidewalk. Chalk was white, sometimes light yellow in grown-up grades, but never in colors so rich and vivid. And now Mrs. Brown was writing, *drawing* a long red box in the center of the board, bleeding deep, shiny lines as bold and tangy as strawberry Kool-Aid.

Do as I do, she said again, and I did, mimicking her bright chalk shapes on my page with pale, waxy imitations in red Crayola. Mrs.

Brown was drawing a wagon! Red rectangle. Black circles for wheels. Brown shaft. Green handle. I was drawing a wagon, too. My picture looked like hers.

Mrs. Brown wrote a large red *S* at the top of my paper. *Satisfactory*, she said. That meant Good, she said. It didn't look as good to me, though, not any more, now that she had written right on the front of my nice drawing. I looked back up at the board. Nobody put a big *S* on her picture. Now they didn't look the same at all.

Lisa, the girl who sat in the space next to me, had drawn a glorious picture, far better in my estimation than my own. Hers was a dark black rectangle filled with circles and triangles and spirals of yellow and green, with a zig-zag red fringe border, blue-purple wheels and a bright orange handle. Lisa was very pleased with her work. Her wagon was different from everyone else's. It was very different from the one in the middle of the blackboard.

Mrs. Brown did not think it was Good. She marked Lisa's paper with a broad, cursive *U*, looping like a deep red cut across the middle of Lisa's wagon. *U*nsatisfactory, Mrs. Brown said, making a big frown. Lisa explained that her picture was prettier than the plain red wagon on the chalkboard. Mrs. Brown said that Lisa would have to learn to *follow directions*. That's what first grade is for.

Lisa took her paper back to her desk, buried her face in her arms, and cried for the rest of the school day. She earned many more U's that year.

I liked Lisa. I liked her very much.

Organ Donor

My second grade teacher was an educator's educator, veteran of more than twenty years' experience maintaining order in front of an elementary school blackboard. Mrs. White's signature maxim was "buckle down and *work*", a nonsensical directive that inexplicably involved the association of a fashion accessory, a gravitational direction, and an undefined activity. I knew from the first day I was in big trouble.

I wasn't the only one. Mrs. White had no idea how much of a professional challenge she was in for. For years she had lobbied the principal to be assigned an "accelerated" class, believing that this was the next logical step in an already noteworthy pedagogical career. That year she got her wish.

Finding no buckles in Mrs. White's classroom, I resigned myself to the drill of daily activities as a monotonous continuation of first grade, with an added sense of disappointment, a feeling I had somehow been lied to, just a little bit. Second grade was as boring as the previous year had been, and just as hot. The long, un-air-conditioned Texas summers lasted well into November, and the clanking classroom radiators that were always turned up too high through the gray winter season kept us sweaty and miserable year round. Fashionable velour pullovers (the first mass-market spin-off from the new Star Trek TV show) and itchy knit dickies that Stepmother tucked into the front of my button-down shirts made things even worse.

As the semester wore on, we grew tired of replicating lower case letters in endless rows of circles and lines, and adding up pictures of pennies, nickels and dimes on the pages of our math workbooks. In reading group, we argued convincingly that all cats, even kittens, say "Meow", and everybody knows it, and therefore the new word "mew" that appeared in our readers was simply mistaken. We howled with laughter when the word 'b-u-t' was added to our vocabulary, and no, we could not be bothered to get back up into our chairs and face forward and stop giggling, even when threatened with a whipping.

We longed for the day when we would be allowed to read real chapter books, and write in cursive like grownups, and why couldn't we just dispense with all of this humdrum stuff and start today? Why couldn't we all sing, or act out a play, or draw pictures, or build a boat?

Mrs. White responded with Divide and Conquer tactics: Seating arrangements were shifted daily, and any unauthorized camaraderie was instantly rewarded with a trip to the Principal's office, or the promise of after-school detention. One empty student desk was moved to the front, next to the teacher, so she could keep a jaundiced, watchful eye on whomever became the Offender of the Day. In a grand show of public humiliation, one student or other would be singled out and force-marched to the front of the class, where he (it was almost always a he) would sit in shame and dishonor, or at least far enough away from the other students to minimize class disruptions.

I spent much of the second grade sitting beside Mrs. White in this manner, picking at the archaeological specimens of chewing gum that had fossilized on the underside of the desk, and peeling perfect sets of fingerprints from hands dipped in shallow pools of Elmer's glue spilled into the desktop pencil groove. Why waste time reading here? We had books at home.

Our home library included a healthy collection of Dr. Seuss and Golden Books, a couple of dictionaries, Dad's student annuals from high school, junior college and university, and a handful of Reader's Digest Condensed Books for grownups. (We had yet to acquire our shining new edition of the 1967 *World Book Encyclo-*

pedia.) This motley collection also included a small but instructive *Guide to Home Health*, complete with chapters on basic human anatomy and organ systems. This was a foreign book, brought into our home by Stepmother, herself a professional educator. Each chapter was illustrated with a classic pen and ink rendering of the organ in question, a detailed cross section of *The Heart, The Lung, The Kidney*, etc.

I loved 'reading' the *Guide to Home Health*, flipping through the pages and counting the growing number of two- and three-letter words that I actually knew: on, it, the. But. Of course I had not developed enough as a reader to interpret any of the text. I had barely learned to hold the letters of the alphabet together in my mind, or comprehend a sentence of four words. But these illustrations captured my attention day after day, for all the afternoon and evening hours that I was supposed to be studying arithmetic. I was enthralled by the lines, and the science they represented.

Here were the secrets of the human body revealed in pictures, diagrams of what people looked like underneath their skins, what you could see if x-ray vision glasses really worked. I studied them endlessly, running my tiny, seven-year-old fingers along each line again and again, as if to Braille the information into my brain. After a while I tried to draw the pictures myself, using a fat elementary school pencil to recreate the illustrator's perfect curves and hatchings on scraps of Big Chief newsprint, or expensive sheets of typing paper borrowed from the box in Dad's desk drawer. These initial graphic experiments ended quickly in failure. The lines were much too thick, the curves were wrong, and soon everything turned into a muddy grey mess.

After some puzzling over the problem, I decided that a project of this magnitude required superior materials, and forbidden techniques. Yes, I would attempt to *trace* these pictures. (Everyone knew tracing was cheating, but it was the only way I could possibly reproduce these splendid images, and study them at my leisure.) To do so, I would need skinny, grown-up pencils, and special see-through paper. These, too, I pilfered from Dad's desk, hoping the loss would not be noticed. It had been a long time since Dad or Stepmother had typed anything. I counted on that trend continuing. At least I had my very own pencil sharpener, with openings for fat *and* skinny pencils. If I took extra care not to break the points, I could keep my materials in working order for a long time without asking for help.

The Heart. The Kidney. The Knee Joint. The Eye. I dutifully traced each of these, line by line, onto carefully scissored half-sheets of onionskin – complete with a curious starburst of narrow, straight lines leading outward in all directions from the organs in question, each ending in a horizontal rule with a big, grown-up word perched above it. These words were beyond my comprehension. I left them off of the pictures.

Not wanting to get caught with expensive pieces of purloined typewriter paper in my possession, I tucked each of the drawings into the inside pocket of my faded blue, cloth-covered snap ring binder, and smuggled them into my desk at school.

Where Mrs. White discovered them.

"Donald, did you do these? Did you draw these pictures?" Mrs. White looked very serious, as she glanced from my eyes to the papers, and back again. I was caught. I might as well admit it, and assume my usual position in the desk at the front of the room.

"Yes, Ma'am," I answered sheepishly.

"My Goodness!" she said. "How long have you been drawing pictures like this?"

I didn't want to say for sure, thinking that if I told her how long I had truly been at it, my punishment would be compounded.

An offense of this magnitude might even earn me a trip to the Principal's office. I resigned myself to the inevitable. "I dunno… A little while, I guess." Take me away.

"Why, they are magnificent!" She exclaimed. "I had no idea you could draw so well!"

Rather than take my pictures and throw them into the trash as I expected, she climbed up on the step stool and thumbtacked them, one by one, onto the long cork border above the black-board, where everyone could see. She even called the class to attention, to show them all what excellent and unexpected work I had done.

Some time after, Dad and Stepmother came home from an evening Parent-Teacher conference, amazed that for once they had received a positive report about me. They could not have been more surprised than I was. They weren't even going to punish me for stealing their expensive onionskin paper.

For a while I was really happy, delighted that something I enjoyed doing this much was actually earning me some positive attention. It still felt a little creepy, though. My usual behavior seldom ended in accolades, and experience had taught me that bad news was waiting for me somewhere, around every corner.

No telling how far away that corner might be, though, so I decided to keep up the good work. I got out my pencil and tracing paper, and started in again. *The Lung. The Hand.* I was busily tracing the metacarpals, holding my tongue steady to keep the lines from overlapping when Stepmother looked in on me.

"What's that you're doing now? Oh, for heaven's sake – *Are you marking in that book!?*"

"No," I replied. "I'm *drawing.*"

"No, you are *not!* I can see from here. You are writing directly on those pages!"

"*No!* I'm..." Frustrated, I moved aside to show her that I was in fact drawing on the onionskin, not the book page itself.

"Oh. I *see* now... So you've been *tracing* these pictures all along?"

(Of *course* I've been tracing them! I'm in the second grade, for God's sake. I've never had an art lesson in my life. Who do you think I am, Michaelangelo? Jr.?)

"Y...yes." This was it.

"So, you *lied* to us," she hissed, squinting her eyes menacingly, sighting down the length of her index finger, pointed straight at my nose. "And to your teacher, who was so proud of you. And to all the other children, too!"

She paused for a moment, while I crumpled inside.

"You should be ashamed of yourself, *shouldn't* you? Why, you made *everyone* think that you actually *drew* these pictures yourself! And on your father's good typing paper, too. Wait 'til he hears about *this!*"

She hurried from the room, leaving me to wait for a repeat performance when Dad arrived. I figured that if I had to wait for the worst, I might as well keep drawing. An hour or more passed, time to finish *The Hand*, and start on *The Bladder*, with its confusing collection of attendant structures. Linear spokes extending from this illustration were labeled with the usual array of complex terms: *Urethra. Scrotum. Penis. Testicle.* None of these words meant anything to me, even if I had been capable of reading them.

By bedtime I had yet to hear from my father. I brushed my teeth and tucked myself in, avoiding the potential wrath of good-night hugs.

***

The next day I presented my latest efforts to Mrs. White, so she could post them along with the others above the blackboard. She was greatly impressed by *The Hand* and *The Lung*, but when she got to *The Bladder*, her expression changed completely.

"Does your mother know you are drawing these things?"

"Sure she does. You talked to her about it during your Parent/ Teacher meeting. She saw me drawing those in my room last night." Well, she *did*.

That day Stepmother made an unexpected visit to our classroom. She did not come to see me. Mrs. White disappeared with her into the Teacher Conference Room, where they spoke quietly among themselves. When Stepmother went home, she left quickly, and took my latest drawing with her.

The next day, the rest of my pictures were taken down from their place of honor over the blackboard, replaced with a decorative strip of colored, corrugated cardboard. I never saw them again. Back home, my beloved *Guide to Home Health* was moved onto a high shelf in Stepmother's closet. Any anatomical curiosity I had was met thereafter with cold imperatives to wait until high school, when I was told I would be old enough to ask such questions. The experience convinced me of a number of Truths, one of which has lasted into my adulthood: *Drawing is Hard. Tracing is Cheating. Artists Don't Get Any Respect*, and *Forbidden Fruit Tastes the Best — even if you don't know it at the time.*

By the time I discovered the Anatomical Man illustrations in the *World Book Encyclopedia*, complete with full-color, see-through overlays, I knew how to read most of the words – and I knew to keep that information to myself.

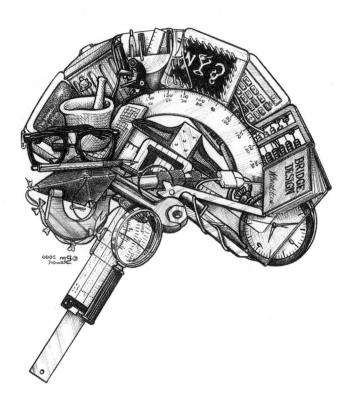

PreMed

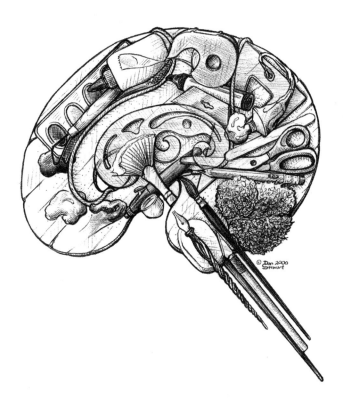

Art 101

> *Two roads diverged in a wood, and I--*
> Robert Frost: The Road Not Taken (1915)

"We've had this conversation before, haven't we? About this time last year, as I recall."

My faculty advisor was not keen on granting my request this time, either.

"Remember, you're on the premedical path here, son," he said. "So far it looks like you're on track, but I don't have to remind you – or maybe I do – that this is a competitive program. Medical schools are looking for good grades in a *solid academic curriculum*. Why do you want to compromise your chances of success by having an art course on your transcript? All this can do is lower your chances of getting in."

Yes, we had had a similar conversation the previous year. I tried to explain to him then that I was fully aware of the negative effect that a basic drawing class might have on my chances of being accepted to medical school. I was also aware that college was probably the last chance I would have to explore art as an academic pursuit. When and where better to do so than here and now, at a liberal arts institution? To my knowledge, there were no art classes listed on the medical school syllabus. I would not have this opportunity again for a long, long time, if ever.

I was prepared to explain this to the admissions committees when the time came to apply to medical school: Art would make me a more well-rounded candidate. The ability to draw would help me with the study of anatomy. Artistic skills would improve my eye-hand coordination, which would be of use in surgery or therapeutic procedures. It would help me interpret x-rays...

I could tell my well-reasoned arguments failed to penetrate his professional skepticism, just as they had failed before. From the counselor's perspective, the choice of art versus science did not really constitute a choice at all. I was here to learn all I could that would prepare me to become a doctor. Learning to draw pictures would be seen as an unnecessary distraction, and if I were serious about a future in medicine, I should get busy selecting my next round of hard-core science courses.

"Let's take a look: we've got Histology, Comparative Anatomy, Biochemistry, Genetics (You're going to have to take Genetics. You know that, right?), Physiology, Botany..."

Yes, I knew that I would have to take these courses. I *wanted* to study these subjects. *All* of them. I actually looked forward to the process of learning about biological organisms and chemical systems. For the time being, however, I was sick of *labs*.

Pre-meds, like students in other major courses of study, were expected to attend lectures, read assigned course material, and prepare for tests. We may have been asked to write a research paper now and then, or complete a class project in return for our final grades. Science majors, however, were also required to complete a full round of laboratory studies, in addition to our regular course work. At least twice a week we reported to Biology Lab, Chemistry Lab, Physics and/or Computer Lab, Botany and Histology and Field Zoology and Genetics and Anatomy and Physiology, *Lab*.

I was still very much interested in my premedical major, completely devoted to medicine as the ultimate career goal. And my grades were good. I wasn't looking for an easy A. Still, I felt like I could use a little breather, a brief change of pace – something that would break the monotony of an endless series of science studies. Art seemed to be the answer. And I *liked* art. What could be wrong with studying something else that I liked?

Since elementary school, I felt an affinity for the creative process, and even believed that I might have some talent along those lines. In middle school I played at watercolor painting, feeding my curiosity and pushing the medium as far as I could without formal instruction. Now, in college, I wanted to get a taste of serious studio art – before it was too late. To do that, I needed the approval of the gatekeeper, my FA. Without his signature, I would not be allowed to enroll in Art 101: *Basic Drawing and Painting for Non-Art Majors*.

"Surely you can see that this art business would be a waste of time," he continued. "Why don't we go ahead and sign you up for Genetics…"

"What is my GPA, sir?" I asked him, interrupting his thought.

"Excuse me?"

"My Grade Point Average. What is my average so far?" He flipped through my academic folder, frowned around the stem of his pipe, raised his eyebrows in surprise. "Four-point-oh, isn't it?" Straight A's. Now I had his attention. "So how about letting me indulge myself for just this one class? Then I'll get back to the science stuff full time."

"I don't know about that," he replied, his skepticism seeming to erode, the tiniest bit, before returning in earnest. "What will *your parents* think of you frittering away their hard-earned money on an art class? They sent you to college to get a real education."

There it was. The Parent card. Surely he had me on this one.

"Actually, sir, *I'm* paying for my education. Shouldn't that give me a vote on the issue?"

It was true. My father had paid for college on his own. The first member of his extended family with an academic degree, he felt that a college education was most appreciated if it were the result of the student's own initiative, beyond sweat equity.

"You can attend whatever college you can afford," he told both of his boys. "*And I expect you to go to college.*"

Through a cobble of scholarships, summer employment, work-study and off-campus jobs, my brother and I would each manage to earn undergraduate degrees with high marks, emerging debt-free and ready for graduate training. I hoped that this demonstration of self-sufficiency would one day carry some weight with the medical school admissions committees. On this particular day, I was hoping it would be enough to convince my Faculty Advisor to let me go *draw*.

With a reluctant sigh, he scratched his initials at the bottom of my new course schedule, and handed the paper to me. At last, I had my ticket to the Art department.

***

"It says here that you are minoring in *art?*"

I had been waiting for the question to come up. My advisor had warned me, after all, hadn't he?

"Not exactly, sir. Originally I just signed up for the non-major's drawing class. They let me take a few extra courses for some of my electives."

"You must be pretty good."

"It was a nice diversion from the academics."

"You need that. If you don't have something to take your mind off work every now and then…"

"I thought it might help in anatomy. I want to be a surgeon. But mostly I just enjoyed it. There probably won't be much time for me to draw over the next few years. Assuming I get accepted, I mean."

"Having a background in the arts certainly won't hurt your chances to get into medical school. On the contrary. These days we're looking for anything that will separate out our more desirable candidates. Every one of you has the GPA for it, or your application wouldn't have been taken seriously."

"Thank you, sir."

"You all have a long list of extracurriculars, too, but frankly those lists are pretty much identical. Anything we can find that will positively differentiate one applicant from another makes the Committee's job that much easier. Heck, last year we accepted a dance major, if you can believe that. I hear she's doing very well in the program."

I could believe it.

My acceptance letter arrived early, just before the start of my senior year. It would be weeks before any of my classmates received theirs.

Sometimes You Punt

I used to kick a football. I used to kick a lot, actually, from sixth grade through junior high and high school, for a while even into college.

Kicking is one of those things a kid can do alone, measuring the results of his own effort, working out his technique and his frustrations without the false empathy or open criticism of a well-meaning friend or brother or parent or coach, each with their own brand of measuring stick, and a cold mental clipboard for keeping score, sometimes for years, sometimes forever.

Team sports never really interested me. As a little league short-stop I spent entire innings marveling at the flow of sand sifting through the webbing of my ball glove. I believed the seventh grade football coach when he screamed to me that I didn't have what it took to move the blocking dummy a goddamned inch, and that I lacked both the *initiative* and *dazaar* to perform at a *hunnert-n-ten percent* for the team. He somehow failed to notice that I also lacked the extra thirty or forty pounds owned by my teammates, along with whatever self-destructive tendencies they had that caused them to crash head first into one another on the coach's orders.

It's not that I lacked an appreciation of physical activity. I liked to run. I practiced martial arts. I danced. I rode my bicycle. I spent days in the woods, climbing rocks and trees, damming creeks, building habitable shelters. I just didn't see any reason to *compete* as a vehicle for achieving physical prowess or athletic excellence. Competition meant facing off with another human being, mea-suring my level of ability against theirs. This idea made very little sense to me. I learned early on that there were going to be people who were better than me at just about anything. Proving that point over and over held no real fascination. On the other hand, finding someone to beat in any kind of competition made no sense, either. The outcome was hopelessly rigged: one person felt terrific, the other defeated. When I lost, I felt bad. When I won, I felt bad for the other guy. Having a trophy to remind me that I had hurt someone else didn't make me feel much like a winner.*

The key to developing athletic skill (or *any* skill, I found), was to identify something I liked to do, and discover ways to become better at it, for however long the process remained enjoyable and challenging. Kicking a football was fun, gratifying, and offered immediate feedback on the success or failure of my efforts.

Technically, I wasn't really a kicker. What I liked to do was *punt* the ball. This is no small distinction: Kicking requires a tee, or somebody else to hold the ball for you, Lucy-style, to your Charlie Brown. Kicking is a structured activity. It requires preparation and teamwork. Kicking is also a *positive* activity. You kick to start the game, to score extra points, and to give the other guys a chance to play after your team makes a touchdown. Kicking is a function of optimism and celebration.

Punting is an acknowledgement of failure. An unavoidable admission of inadequacy. You punt on the fourth down, when your team has screwed up three out of four chances to move the ball down the field. A punt is a chance to save face, an attempt to pull your team out of a hole of its own digging. A last-ditch effort to make up for multiple past failures. Nonetheless, if that's where you find yourself, it seems sensible to give as good a showing as you can.

Punting is a solitary activity. No tee. No ball holder. You're on your own.

---

*(Defeating someone who is trying to do me harm is another matter altogether. Then it's no-holds-barred, and winner-take-all. Just because I don't like to compete doesn't make me a doormat.)

Start from a standing position. One, two eager steps to build forward momentum, extend the ball out and away, a few degrees to the left, laces up. Right hand to hold, left to guide, release with both hands at once, Goldilocks fashion: Not too soon, not too late.

A well-punted football leaves the foot with a rolling motion, tip pointed upward at exactly forty-five degrees, spinning along the axis of the spheroid, no wobble, like a well-thrown pass. The perfect punt has all of these qualities, and one more: If executed properly, the ball will rise to the apex of its flight, then flatten its trajectory briefly before tipping over in a seamless roll, its point rifling along a clean parabolic path to the ground.

A less-than-perfect punt will fail in the rollover phase. The football sails up beautifully, but maintains an up-tilted attitude as gravity begins to coax it back to earth. Spinning in place, the ball now presents a maximum surface area to wind resistance, changing instantly from a bullet to a brick. Rather than describe the maximum symmetrical arc of a parabola, the football stalls in mid-air, and drops, half way to its intended destination.

A flick of the toe is all it takes to make or ruin the path of a beautifully punted football. A slight misstep, an error in cadence, a slip of the fingers on release, and the entire effort is undone. I spent hours working on my punting technique, dissecting the process, identifying pitfalls, polishing the steps, timing, position, release, follow-through. When I was comfortable with the results, I started training myself to do it left-footed.

This all amounted to wonderful physical conditioning, improved eye-hand coordination, and a tremendous boost to my self-esteem. Once or twice it even caught the attention of the high school coaches, who would find me practicing on the football field after school, while the team was working out in the weight room.

Fortunately they never took my ability seriously. I was too small, they said, and wasn't serious about kicking for the team, anyway. Wasn't willing to give a hunnert-n-ten percent.

Only once did I try to punt the ball during a football game, in college, on the intramural squad. My classmates had noticed me practicing one day, executing a series of seamless, 60- to 75-yard rifled bullets, each ending in a forward bounce toward the end zone. They recruited me on the spot, handed me a jersey, and sent me into a game of sandlot ball against a rival fraternity.

What could possibly go wrong?

Brimming with confidence, I took my place well behind the center, caught the snap, stepped forward rhythmically, and looked up to see a writhing wall of angry college men bearing down on me, intent on doing me immediate harm. Still I focused, made pinpoint contact, and felt the satisfying arc of energy leave my leg and foot, sending the football sailing high into the air.

Straight up into the air, it turned out. What might have been another 75-yarder instead tracked vertically, a path easily monitored from my flattened position on the dusty field. A gust of wind cradled the ball at the crest of its narrow arc, then carried it *backwards* a full ten yards. The opposing team recovered and scored, amid howls of laughter from my own side, laced liberally with well-earned accusations and epithets.

No longer the hero, I limped from the field confirmed and strengthened in my solitary belief that contact sports were misguided adventures at best.

Once every few years my left knee still locks up briefly, pops painfully back into place, and reminds me of a time when I left my convictions on the sidelines, and mis-stepped into the competitive arena.

Anchors Aweigh

I tried to enlist in the Navy to get a free ride through medical school.

Seemed like a good idea at the time. Tuition paid. Monthly stipend. I could go to school, buy a small condo, build equity while I built a career.

The recruiter was happy to hear from me. Yes, if I could drive to the nearest military base, someone would meet me for processing. Welcome aboard!

Everything went well, until we got to the medical part of my processing: They failed me on the vision test.

It seems I cannot perceive depth. At all. Period. It's quite possible I never could - something about different focal lengths in each eye.

Do I wear glasses?

Not anymore. I did for a while, when I was six or seven, to straighten out a lazy eye.

They showed me the test again, this small white box with dull metal bars placed inside, some wide, some narrow, matte black kalimba keys spaced at varying distances from the little square window in front.

When I looked in the window, all I saw were vertical lines, flat black stripes standing side by side, no sense whatsoever that some were standing closer to the opening, others farther away.

The corpsman gave me three regulation tries, three long chances to tell him which of the bars he had placed in front of the others.

Sorry. All I saw was lines.

The corpsman rearranged the bars once more, and told me to try again. *Look carefully.* If I guessed correctly, he said, he would pass me on the test.

Lines. I saw black lines. That's all.

He suggested that I did not understand how important it was that I pass this test. How essential it was to my future in the Navy. Without a passing report, he said, they would never let me pilot a plane.

Okay. I still only saw lines.

Try one more time. Try *real hard.*

Lines.

Too bad. I would never be a pilot, could never be a flight surgeon. I'd probably never make it past Lieutenant.

That's cool, I said. I'm just here for the scholarship, not the career. I might not be able to perceive depth, but that didn't mean I completely lacked perspective.

Pulling a dismissive, all but disgusted face, he scrawled across my report in bold marker: Failed. X 3. Then he told me to wait for the doc, for a full physical.

***

A while later the doctor walked in. He was not in uniform, just a shirt and tie. He told me he was retired. They brought him back to the base from time to time to help out with this sort of thing.

The rest of my physical exam was normal: Chicken pox, Check. Measles, Check. Broken arm, age eight: No sequelae. Sit down. Raise your arms. Breathe. Stand up. Turn your head and cough.

This part of the evaluation took half as much time as the vision test. I guess things just take longer when they're trying so hard to make you pass.

No, my bad eyesight wouldn't keep me from getting the military scholarship. Not surprising, really, since it never kept me from doing anything else I wanted to do. Good thing I never wanted to fly fighter jets.

I asked the doc whether he had any advice for me. "Sure," he said. "Don't volunteer for anything. Ever. Just show up and do your job."

"How come?" I wondered out loud.

"Listen, son. You volunteer, you get more work. No more pay. Just more work. Try and get through your tour without calling attention to yourself. That way you don't get shot down."

"So I guess the worst that can happen is, you get assigned extra duty anyway."

"Not hardly. Worst that can happen is you sign up for some kind of extra training, then decide you can't cut it. Or you just don't want to."

"So they don't they let you quit if it's not working out?"

"Oh, they let you quit all right. But there's nothing in the military worse than a *Quitter*." He stopped to light a cigarette. "You quit at something, son, and you're marked a Shit Bird ever after."

He could tell I was wondering.

"A *Shit Bird*. That's a bird that doesn't do anything useful, just stands around on a post and shits. Someone who's worthless to the military. When you're a Shit Bird, they treat you like shit. They give you extra shit duty. No more breaks, no more favors. You're just marking time until you're discharged. And that's time you don't want to spend in any man's Navy."

I thanked him for his insights.

"Just keep your head down, son."

***

As soon as the doctor finished signing my medical forms, I was ushered over to headquarters to formalize my enlistment.

"Do you have any questions?" my recruiter asked, shuffling a sheaf of papers together into an even stack.

I did. I asked about the usual things: How much time would I spend in military training while in med school? How much time is served on board ship? How was being a Navy doc different from civilian practice? Could a nurse who outranked me countermand my medical orders? That sort of thing.

"Speaking of payback time – once this is all said and done, exactly how many years of service will I owe the Navy?"

"That depends on how many years we support you in your education."

"Okay, assuming four years of med school, and five years of surgery residency, that would be nine years. The recruiter I talked to on the phone told me it would be one year for each year paid for by the Navy, plus two years additional. So eleven years. On the other hand, if I go right to work after medical school, it would be six years total. Is that correct?"

"That would be determined by the circumstances."

"I don't understand. Was he wrong about the formula?"

"We look at each case individually."

"Okay, then… let's keep it simple. If I go right to work after graduating from medical school, it would be six years total payback. Is that correct?"

"Well, not necessarily. You will agree that a graduating medical student is not qualified to treat patients…

That was news to me.

"So you're saying that I have to do my surgical residency while I'm in the service. Does that count as payback, or add extra years to my obligation?"

"The Navy will assess its needs during your training. If there is a military residency available in your preferred specialty, you may be able to serve part of your obligation there."

"And if there isn't?"

"You may be able to defer your service obligation while you undergo approved civilian residency training."

Now things were getting complicated. "I *may* be able to defer my service obligation? How will I know for sure?"

"That would be determined by the circumstances."

"Okay, work with me here. Let's say I still want to be a surgeon, but I'm willing to put that off until I fulfill my military service obligation. I graduate from medical school, then train for one year in a general internship, on a military base. Can I then sign on to active duty? How many years will I owe under those circumstances? Six years?"

"That would be a reasonable assumption, provided the Navy is still in need of your skills at that time."

"Are you telling me that there is a possibility that the Navy might *not* be in need of my services?"

"Manpower assessments are always in a state of flux. It's impossible to predict the future."

"So, if there's a cutback, and all of a sudden the Navy doesn't need doctors, what happens then? You guys can just cut off my funding?"

"Hypothetically, that could happen, I guess."

"Hypothetically, what would happen *then*?"

"You would be responsible for recompensing the Navy for their investment."

"Wait - I would have to pay the Navy *back*?"

"Hypothetically."

"Hypothetically, that would suck."

I could see myself getting half way through medical school, two years into a 30-year mortgage, then have my funding jerked out from under me.

"So I'm half way through medical school, two years into a 30-year mortgage, then my funding gets jerked out from under me?"

"That would be a worst-case scenario."

"But then I would have to drop out of medical school. I'd be unemployed, with two years of tuition, and a house to pay for. And no medical career in my future."

He said nothing.

"At least I wouldn't owe the Navy any pay back time. Wait... I wouldn't owe the Navy any pay back time, right?"
"That would be determined by the circumstances."

"So what you're saying is, there is no scenario I can come up with that will allow you to tell me what my term of service will be."

"At some point you'll just have to trust us."

"You're kidding, right? Good God, you *have* to be kidding! You're asking me to place my future – and my life – into your hands. Sorry, sir, but if you can't tell me the rules of the game before we start to play, I'd be a fool to run out onto the field, wouldn't I?"

"You said that you wanted to serve your country."

"I'm still willing to serve my country, only right now you haven't convinced me that my service is answering a pressing need. You say you want to assist me in developing my talents, yet you aren't willing to tell me how much that's going to cost me."

"As I said, that would be determined..."

"By the circumstances. Yeah, I got that. Why not just say up front that once I sign that document, my release date from the Navy is entirely arbitrary. If we were at war, that might make some sense. But we're not at war. So this is really a straightforward business negotiation. And from where I'm looking, it's a pretty bad deal."

"I'm sure there's some way we could come to an understanding…"

Great.

When you fellas get this all figured out, let me know.

A Familiar Face

In the Emergency Room we heard the most unbelievable stories, only to see our share of them crash through the doors on Friday and Saturday nights, and land torn and pulsing into our laps. Urban legends come to life: the predictable consequences of fireworks, drain cleaners, unloaded handguns, broken glass and razor blades, a laundry list of items lodged deep in private recesses (and stranger still, detailed protocols for removing them), knives and nails and crowbars embedded in talking heads, the one rule being to leave things in place until you get the patient to the operating room.

My most moving ER experience happened before I was even out of college. The director of the new Emergency Department at the Southern School of Medicine had invited me to come and observe his practice for a day or two, to see if this sort of thing was what I really wanted to do with my life, rather than make a career out of my summer apprenticeship at the steel mill. It was a fortuitous visit, and one that certainly brought an end to my interest in the construction industry. It may also have begun the unraveling of my plans to become a doctor.

Around four in the afternoon an ambulance barked to a stop in the entryway. Attendants flung the doors open and rushed in with a silver mannequin strapped to the gurney. The nurses descended on a figure that looked for all the world like the Tin Man from the Wizard of Oz.

Six-foot even, a hundred and seventy-eight pounds, late teens or early twenties, he was covered with silver paint from head to steel-booted toe. If it weren't for the torn tee shirt and painter's pants, one might be persuaded that this fellow spent his days standing in the park, a mime pretending to be a statue.

The story we got from the paramedic was that this guy had fallen from a water tower. The young man had been painting the huge tank with a high-pressure sprayer, when a rope supporting the platform slipped loose and dumped him seventy-five feet to the ground. The only thing that saved him was an oak tree that met him halfway, and broke his fall - along with his pelvis, his wrist, his humerus, and a couple of ribs. After a seven story descent he was lucky - really lucky - to be alive at all.

"Hey, this guy looks like *you*!" one of the nurses noted, smiling up at me while she checked the patient for pupillary responses. It was true. The paint that covered his face in a metallic monotone, combined with the flaccidity of unconsciousness served to erase most of the features that might otherwise have distinguished this man from others of similar age and body type - myself, for example. In silvery profile, his aquiline nose and prominent forehead could have placed him seamlessly within a line-up of the cousins on my mother's side, or just as easily between my brother and me at the dinner table. This was a coincidence that I found more than a little unnerving.

His driver's license revealed that underneath the argent patina, we had the same eye and hair color. Even stranger, we had the same initials, and according to his chart, the same birthday. This man was exactly one year older than I was – and we both had day jobs that involved walking in high places wearing heavy boots and hard hats, and safety belts that usually weren't attached to anything safe.

It's a funny thing, seeing yourself stretched out in effigy on a hospital exam table, getting your arms and neck and chest cut open for the passage of needles and yards of plastic tubing, thinking that you don't yet know enough to tell if you're going to make it out of the room alive.

I learned that day to identify with my patients on a very personal level, a level that I believe served them well in the years that followed, even as the lesson robbed me of the emotional detachment that I would need to protect myself from the challenges of the profession I was determined to pursue. Whether or not that was the lesson the universe was trying to teach me through this curious confluence of events remains an open and valid question. Perhaps I should have paid even closer attention, and learned either to detach myself more effectively, or taken the cue to leave medicine sooner than later.

I never learned what became of this patient. His youth and vitality would surely have served him well in recovering from his broken bones. Whether or not he ever woke up is another question – and if he did, how much of him made the trip back to consciousness is anybody's guess. If medical training were to convince me of anything, it would be that no outcome is ever guaranteed. You do everything you can, and hope for the best, but you can never know what the future holds. For anyone.

Med School

The Association
MS-I*, Day 1: Orientation

It had been a busy morning. 110 of us, mostly strangers, gathered together for the first time in a cavernous, electronically outfitted lecture theatre, the room that would be our academic headquarters for the coming year. Oriented to the freshman medical course syllabus, school history, and the student Code of Conduct, we were shuffled about in alphabetical groups of ten or twenty, taken on tours of the facility, photographed for posterity, given our official ID badges, and guided through a brief tutorial on procedure and etiquette in the cadaver lab.

Collected again in the front of the building for a full class portrait, we were finally herded back into the lecture hall, and dismissed for lunch. The first half of our first day as medical students was done. Just one more thing, though, before we went, if we had a moment, and didn't mind paying attention to an important *unofficial* message, brought to us by a future colleague, entirely on our behalf, and in our own best interests. Thank us.

With all due respect we were introduced to one Johndoe Ossopod, III, M.D., esteemed local surgeon, alumnus of our own Southern School of Medicine, a man with a busy private practice and some stature in the community.

"Ladies and Gentlemen, I am *proud* to have been given the *honor* of *addressing* you today. As your regional representative of our national *Medical Association*, I have been asked to come before you to *encourage* you to join this *august* group."

*MS-I: Medical Student, First Year

The good doctor's casual smile and unctuous demeanor were calculated to set us all at ease, an intention subtly underscored by his saccharine southern drawl.

"While We** *realize* that for the vast majority of you that this is already a *done deal*, a conclusion *foregone* which therefore hardly merits discussion *a'tall*, it *occurs* to us that *some* among you might not in fact know to *join* our organization, if you were not previously *informed* of this necessity, and extended at the very *least* a cordial and *direct invitation* to come on bo-ard *with* us.

"As I am *certain* you already know, the Association is the *only* organization that represents the political and *financial* interests of *you*, the *physician*, in our nation's capital. Indeed, it is the *only* institution that gives you a clear and *powerful voice* in Washington, in support of *your concerns* and *values*. In short, our Association is the *bulwark* that protects and *assures* you the *full measure* of *compensation* for your education, and your *manifold* contributions to society."

Compensation? This was the reason we should join? What about our *patients*?

"Yes, this fine medical organization is the *sole* representative body working on *your behalf*, in order to keep your hard-earned *patient care dollars* out of the hands of a *host* of *pseu*-do-medical practitioners – *charlatans,* if you will, who represent your *competition* in the healthcare marketplace! Once you have *graduated* this fine institution, and completed your residency training, you will be *competing* with a *legion* of naturopaths, homeopaths, herbalists, *po*-diatrists, acupuncturists, chi-ro-practors, *osteopaths*, palm readers, voodoo hooligans, and all manner of *ne'er-do-wells* who will, given the *slightest* opportunity, reach *into* your very own pockets, and *deprive* you of the *income* you have worked so hard to *acquire*, and which is in fact *rightfully yours*.

**The royal We, apparently.

"The only way to *avert* this *unfortunate* potential outcome is to continue to *legislate* these people out of the *market...*"

Income. The *market.* Not a word about patient care. Not a thought about advocacy. Nothing about research, or the importance of our sacred craft, or advancing the state of the art. Nary a mention of improving the quality of healthcare on a national scale, or even in our own communities.

It was all about the money. And I was genuinely surprised.

"Now if you would each take a *brief* moment to step up here at the *dais,* in order to sign the appropriate *forms...* "

Having received the call, the entire class rose from their seats. Nearly all queued up immediately at the front of the room like cattle at a feed trough, hastily signing up, and signing on to the plan that would protect their future incomes.

Only a handful of us declined, a fact ignored for thirty years by the Association. For the remainder of my training, and the entirety of my non-medical career they have successfully tracked my movements across the country, and continued to send me annual invoices (not invitations or solicitations, but actual *bills*) for my outstanding membership dues.

I have never enrolled in their program, never asked for my name to be placed on their mailing list. For their part, the group has never asked for my opinion about national health care, the working conditions of resident physicians, the availability of affordable health insurance, the ethics of advertising life-threatening drugs on television, or the medical challenges of an aging populace. But they do want my money.

At least they were honest about their intentions from the beginning.

Skinner Box

Hi Backatcha!

Got your letter.

How is medical school going? Is it hard? What's it like?

Thanks for asking.

1. *Okay.* 2. *The jury's still out, but yeah.* 3. *I'll tell you:*

Back in college we learned about a thing called a Skinner Box.
This ingenious apparatus was built by some psychologist named
Skinner as a way to torture, that is, *study* rats. He wanted to see,
among other things, how the little guys "responded to stimuli".

Basically, the bottom of the box was made of wire mesh that was
hooked up to an electrical current. To shock the rat. Put rat in
box, flip switch, watch rat jump. Skinner discovered that pretty
much every time you shocked a rat, it jumped. Brilliant guy, this
Skinner. Shock, jump. Shock, jump.

Now, to liven up the experiment (this *was* science, after all), Skinner un-wired half of the floor, creating a little "shock free" zone
where the rat could rest, and not get zapped again. Lo and Be-
hold, the rats preferred to stay on the non-electrified side. They
did not like getting shocked.

Only trouble was, the rat's food dish was on the other side of
the box, across the electrified floor. Go out for a bite to eat, get
shocked again – the rat equivalent of a huge bill at a fancy restaurant. It didn't take long for the rats to decide they would rather go
on a diet, only crossing over when they got really, *really* hungry.

Of course Skinner then had to up the ante, so he re-wired the whole thing again, and started shocking *both* sides of the floor at random intervals, just to see what would happen to the hungry rats. And guess what? They *jumped!* Every time he hit the switch, just like before. Zap the right side, they jump left. Zap left, they jump right. Amazing. Whatever the experiment proved, at least it solved the food problem. The rats were too busy jumping to eat.

To his amazement, Skinner found that if he zapped the poor critters hard enough for long enough, eventually the rats would just lie down and take the shocks, until eventually they starved to death.

That's what the psych folks call *Learned Helplessness:* If things get bad and stay that way, eventually you figure there's not a damned thing you can do about it. You just take it til you die.

Medical school is a lot like a Skinner Box.

Work hard, and they shock you. (I'm studying harder than I ever did in college, and I have yet to make a solid A on a single test here. In any class.)

Try and get a little rest, and they *really* shock you. The work piles up fast, and it's very easy to fall behind. Lectures, labs, lectures. Every day builds relentlessly on yesterday's material. And everything's new. Take time to sit back and digest what you've just crammed in to your brain, and you've already missed today's lesson. Which is essential to understanding tomorrow's lesson.

The whole system is designed to make you fail, and if you aren't failing, to make you think you are. Or that you already have. As long as they keep you in mortal fear of losing your dream, you keep at it, shock or no shock.

And that's probably better than taking time out to try and under-

stand what's really happening. Like last weekend when I had to
study for two tests. Physiology & Histology. I studied my ass off
for the last histology test, and made a high C. Screw it, I thought.
Study for the Fizz test instead. Histology barely gets a passing
glance. Result? I bombed the physiology, and came closest yet to
an A in Histo.

What have we learned here? *Don't waste your time studying.*

Sounds silly, I know, but trust me: In this environment, shock
and reward have nothing to do with effort. Causality is a fiction,
except for this: *If* you stop and think about it, *then* you derail
yourself. If you stop studying altogether, then you *will* fail the
program. You can't win, but you can surely fail. The only upside
is that if you fail rarely enough, they may let you move on to the
next level. Success is a lie, but progress remains a tantalizing possibility. The only way is forward. So we keep at it, day after day,
hoping that somehow we will jump through enough hoops to become doctors. The alternative is unthinkable. There is no plan B.

So how are things going with you?

Private Practice

As an eager third year medical student, I was awe-struck, sitting in the *private office* of a prominent young pediatrician. This was the first day of my community medicine rotation, and I was sure to be there early, not wanting to miss a minute of this opportunity.

Balanced on the edge of my seat, my admiring attention was riveted on the array of diplomas and certificates on the wall behind his desk: Magna cum Laude. Phi Beta Kappa. Alpha Omega Alpha. Chief Resident. Prestigious Research Fellowship. Diplomate, American Board of Pediatrics. *Wow.* This guy had scored at every level.

I had lobbied hard to get this assignment. Dr. Jungman was a rock star in pediatric circles, five years after he left his *second* tour as Chief Resident, convinced to stay on because he was so capable, and so loved by administrators, staff, students and patients. His reputation had followed him into a successful community practice, and grew as he attracted the attention and approval of affluent parents with notable pedigrees of their own. And here I was, about to follow in his long shadow, if only for a day.

I sat in his office, absorbing the aura, puzzled by the only item that seemed out of place: a ceramic ashtray at the far corner of his cluttered desk. It was full of cigarette butts. I mean *full.* Easily three or four packs of spent, smashed filters piled in a domed mass, the refuse of the previous day's carcinogenic inhalations.

This was a little disconcerting. In those days, a smoking habit of that magnitude was not unheard of. Your average fifty-year-old male patient probably had a similar story noted in the Social History of his medical record. But this was a young guy. A smart guy. A *doctor*'s doctor. He knew the risks associated with cigarette smoking.

He knew *better.*

As I was pondering the ramifications of this discovery, Jungman walked in, introduced himself, plopped down behind his desk, and mashed out his cigarette. He promptly lit up another.

It was only nine a.m., and he looked like he had already put in a full day on the job. Pale and haggard, his face pulled into a smirking frown, his brow permanently creased, he looked a decade older than his thirty-something years. I assumed he had been up all night working with critically ill patients.

"Sorry I'm late," he said. "Got pulled over for speeding this morning. Hope I didn't keep you waiting too long."

I assured him that he had not.

"*Cop actually pulled me over and gave me a ticket,*" he continued. "Couldn't believe it! I *told* him I was on my way to the hospital."

He shuffled through his desk drawers, found an open roll of antacids, and popped two tablets in his mouth. "Time was the cops left us docs alone. Everything's changed nowadays. Whatcha gonna do."

"This must be an exciting job," I queried, noting his superior academic credentials.

"It pays the bills."

"What I mean is, you must see some interesting clinical presentations." I told him I was really looking forward to shadowing him for the day. "With your background, you must get some complicated referrals."

"Not if I can help it," he replied. "After a while you get tired of waking up at three in the morning to manage some kid with ketoacidosis*. You get to where all you want to see is a room full of sore bellies, runny noses and diarrhea. Routine stuff. Nowadays, we turf the train wrecks over to the university, let hotshots like you figure 'em out."

"So you don't miss that kind of academic challenge?"

"Boy, the new and shiny wore off of this job a long time ago."

"Then why do you still do it?"

"Wife wants a new Mercedes."

"That's it?" I asked, a little too incredulously.

"Ain't that enough? Let's get to work."

He was right. There was very little of the new and shiny left in this man's practice. We spent the day looking at miserable children with runny noses and sore bellies, and exhausted mothers who had been up all night mopping puddles of diarrhea and vomit.

These volatile symptoms weren't the only things that followed me home at the end of the day. With them I carried a newfound resolve to do something – anything – other than open my own private medical practice.

The educational process was working.

* Ketoacidosis: A critical complication of diabetes.

Suicide Notes

As part of our brief introduction to Clinical Psychiatry, all medical students were asked to complete the well-known Minnesota Multiphasic Personality Inventory, a 500-question mega-test designed to define an individual's personality traits and identify potential mental disorders. We were obliged to take the test in its entirety, in order to give us a first-hand understanding of the process, and to learn how answers to seemingly innocuous questions, taken in the proper clinical context, could lead to important diagnostic insights with regard to our future psychiatric patients. The test also gave medical school administrators a covert look into the psychological makeup of their students – an important part of the exercise that they didn't bother to mention to us.

A day or two after finishing the exam, I was called in to discuss the findings. *This should be fun*, I thought. *How often do you get to take a peek inside your own skull?* I reported to the psychologist's office with an attitude of open curiosity and enthusiasm, which rendered me totally unprepared for what was about to happen.

As expected, the MMPI revealed much about me that ordinarily lay quietly concealed beneath the surface of my personality. First, the test said that I was prone to tell *the truth*. To a fault, actually. To the extent, in fact, that under normal circumstances (we didn't get much into what those circumstances might be), I might be considered a compulsive liar. Or a sycophant. Or just honest. In the interest of time and more pressing concerns, we decided to go with honest.

I also scored rather far onto the feminine side of the Masculine-Feminine scale. What did this mean? Well, it could mean that I enjoyed floral arrangements and housework and art museums.

That would make sense, I told the counselor (honestly), given
that I in fact did like flowers and art (didn't everybody?), and that
even though it wasn't very high on my list of preferred activities,
I really didn't mind doing housework. Then I told him that my
grandfather had been a farmer and a florist, and growing up in a
family that consisted of a single father with two sons, it was no
surprise that I could wash dishes and sew on a button.

Of course the high femininity score could also mean that I was
gay. Did I want to talk about that? *(Not really, thanks.)* Am I sure?
(Pretty sure.) It could be important. *(No, it's cool.)*

Did I like boys? It's okay if I did. It's fine if I'm a little uncomfortable talking about it, too. If I didn't feel like admitting such
tendencies that day, I could feel free to schedule a personal appointment to discuss my sexual orientation any time I felt con-
flicted. Any time. Really. Here's his card, just in case. Call him.

Aside from my candidness and sense of aesthetic appreciation,
there was another dramatic condition that was uncovered by the
exam, and it was a Deusie:

I was about to kill myself.

Now this one was serious, he said. The computerized mechanism
that automatically scored the exam sheets had flagged me as a
suicide risk, because of my affirmative answers to the MMPI's
hidden 'alert' questions. It turns out that there are at least three
such questions included in the test, designed specifically to trip up
subjects with the potential to do themselves harm. I had landed
three for three - a hat trick!

This was a *big* problem – and my apparent lack of concern meant
the problem was even worse than they feared. From the dour
look on the counselor's face, I could tell we were in for long ses-
sion. There was a bottom to this, and we had to get to it.

The fact that I had absolutely no intention of orchestrating my own demise carried no weight in the discussion. This was the MMPI. These were the *suicide* questions. These are the red ink dots printed right here on the score sheet, one dot beside each of the three *alert* items. Just take a look at this one:

'I have considered suicide in the past.' True or False?

True. What rational individual entering a life-and-death profession hasn't given the idea long and serious consideration? (Not many, it turns out.)

The psychologist was worried. I wasn't.

Did I have suicidal *ideations*, he wanted to know – meaning, could I imagine the details of taking my own life?

Sure. I certainly had a great imagination, and by age twenty I had seen enough movies and read enough cheap detective novels to come up with a dozen different ways to off myself, with variations on every theme. After an intense series of courses in human anatomy, physiology and pharmacology, that number had easily risen to thirty or forty. Who among us wasn't able to come up with a viable plan, or several, at the drop of a hat? (Again, apparently, not many.) *Why not? Weren't they paying attention?*

Do you believe you have a legitimate reason to kill yourself? *Doesn't everybody?* Dude, if crime, war, drugs, glaring social inequality, fringe religions, global famine, educational loans, disco, the nuclear arms race and this new AIDS plague don't scare the living shit out of you, you have to be pretty dim. Ten minutes of random TV news are excuse enough for anyone to opt out of this program. I wouldn't blame anybody for punching their own ticket, any time they felt good and ready. In fact, there are times when it seemed like the only reasonable thing to do!

Do you feel like killing yourself right now? *Probably not, but if you keep bugging me with these stupid questions, it might start to sound like a good idea.*

In the end, they decided we were dealing with a difference in semantics, and I was probably not at imminent risk of self-destruction. The test said I was not depressed or paranoid, which was good, but I had a mild tendency toward introversion, and that unhealthy penchant for truth-telling still had everyone a little bit concerned.

If I ever needed to talk about things, anything at all, the counselor would be there for me. Any time.

Honest.

The Ethics of Abuse

All students at the Southern School of Medicine were obliged to attend and pass a course in Medical Ethics. This was a relatively new and untested addition to the curriculum, a 1980's response to thirty years of postwar diagnostic and therapeutic developments, which by then were starting to generate a host of unplanned economic challenges, increased government scrutiny, and growing levels of public concern.

For the first time in history, effective treatments for heart disease, diabetes and other maladies of maturity were allowing patients to live well beyond their seventies, though often at the expense of quality of life. A hundred years of cigarette smoking was taking its harsh toll on the ranks of our Greatest Generation, leading to heated debates within and outside of the medical community regarding the practicality of tobacco regulations. People exposed to 1950's - era cosmetic X-ray therapy, like those who dealt with radiation, asbestos, and other noxious substances in the workplace, were turning up with a laundry list of environmental illnesses, plotting a long learning curve of the dangers associated with technological advancement. Thalidomide babies had reached maturity, and they and others were lending their voices to the dialogue surrounding the unpredictable outcomes of modern pharmaceutical therapy.

Lessons learned on the battlefields of Viet Nam were suddenly allowing emergency personnel to save many trauma victims who would certainly have died a generation before, but who were now left waiting for technology and social attitudes to catch up and deal with the range of disabilities arising from these same life-saving interventions. And while the Supreme Court's decision in *Roe v. Wade* was already a decade old, the battle lines for and against abortion – and its ethical cousins euthanasia and assisted suicide – were only then being drawn in courtrooms and hospital corridors across the country.

Hospital administrators and private practitioners were also beginning to come to terms with the mixed blessing of managed care. Health Maintenance Organizations and DRG's (Diagnosis Related Groups, among the first attempts by insurance companies to codify medical procedures and regulate payments) had just been instituted, forcing doctors to grapple with the concepts and consequences of cost containment, and to justify tests and treatments that they routinely ordered for their patients.

On the other side of the ledger, malpractice cases (and associated insurance premiums) were skyrocketing, giving rise to a new era of defensive medicine. Substance abuse was on the rise both in and out of the hospital, and sexual indiscretions in the clinical workplace, previously swept under the rug, were beginning to garner attention, scrutiny, and legal consequence.

The Medical Ethics course was supposed to give us the tools we would need to deal with this gathering storm of clinical, social, and medico-legal ambiguity. It was a Pass/Fail class; apparently earning a P grade meant that we were equal to the task.

Against this miasmic social/political /medical/legal backdrop, a select group of area physicians were invited to come and speak to our Ethics class. Invited was putting it nicely. In fact they were obligated to see us, in order to fulfill the public service provisions of the various plea agreements that allowed them to maintain their medical licenses, which had been placed on probationary status due to recent charges and admissions of substance abuse.

Five professional-looking people, men and women, filed through the door and behind a long folding table placed in the front of the lecture hall. Each was dressed conservatively. They all sat up straight and tall, looking clear-eyed and businesslike and responsible.

And of course, sober.

Four doctors and one nurse, each began to tell us their stories, informing us of the perils and temptations that lay ahead for the rest of us in the medical profession: The OB/Gyn who started drinking in college, and kept up the habit through medical school, residency, and right on into his practice; the nurse who became addicted to pills after hurting her back, lifting a heavy patient; the anesthesiologist who began experimenting with recreational inhalants, then graduated to injectable narcotics, because they were available, and he had problems at home.

They didn't think it could happen to them, but it did, they said. And it could happen to us, too. Their addictions cost them their jobs, their families and their fortunes. Only the intervention of this progressive new rehabilitation program allowed them to retain a measure of dignity along with the remnants of their tattered careers, and the hope that soon they would be able to pull their lives all the way back on track.

They were all now resolute, and confident that this would be the case. All but one.

Somehow one of the speakers seemed slightly out of place that day. Like his compatriots he was well groomed and professionally attired, though among the group he was the only one not wearing a tie, or a suit coat.

He looked young, compared to the others, almost innocent, his face shrouded with a veil of sadness. Slightly built, thin but fit, he moved with a grace that in other contexts would have pegged him for a dancer.

He spoke softly to us, in a tired voice, evidently exhausted from his long struggle with addiction, and the effort of having to negotiate his new life.

"I'm 34 years old," he began. "All I ever wanted to be was a doctor. I worked hard in high school, made straight A's, and, as I'm sure the vast majority of you did, I was inducted into the National Honor Society. As a pre-med in college I studied hard and earned a 3.9 grade average, ODK, and Phi Beta Kappa*. I succeeded, like each of you, in the competitive application process, and was accepted into medical school… where I was shocked to learn that as new physicians-in-training we were *not* to be congratulated for our achievements and welcomed into the fraternity of healers, but instead would be castigated daily in a completely arbitrary and senseless effort to break us down, perpetuating an environment of competition within a class of people who, I thought, should have been learning to work together, as colleagues.

"In spite of that, I continued to work hard, and make good grades. I served as a class officer, and was even elected to AOA**. If there was a credential missing from my student transcript, I couldn't tell you what it was.

"It wasn't until I was all the way into my residency that I was finally able to call up the courage to challenge a professor who was beating us up one day on hospital rounds. I said, 'Excuse me, sir, but is there any point in our training when we can expect to be treated like adults? We've worked really hard to get this far, and it doesn't seem entirely out of line to receive a modicum of respect from those of you whose job it is to instruct us. I mean, a word of encouragement would go a long way. Is that really too much to ask?'

"His response was to ignore my question, by ignoring me, completely. He moved on down the hall to the next patient's room, and expected me to follow along with the rest."

---

* Undergraduate academic honorary societies.
** Alpha Omega Alpha, the honorary society for medical students

The big room fell silent. Even the knuckleheaded geniuses up in the back row, who were known to serve cocktails during lectures, were uncharacteristically attentive.

"I don't know if this was precisely when I began taking drugs, but I do know that this was when I really came to understand that the educational process wasn't at all concerned about me, or about making good doctors. It was all about playing some kind of crazy game. The learning didn't matter. The patients didn't matter. All that mattered was competing and scoring points.

"Ironically, it was the drugs that allowed me to keep playing the game. I didn't become a better doctor, just more effective at doing what was expected of me, in the context of this illusion. They helped me play the role, that's all. I didn't take drugs to get high or even to get away, just to get better at the game. I hated that.

"Now that I'm sober, I find that I still haven't figured out how to fit in, anywhere in the system. I'm not in jail any more, and that's a good thing, but I no longer have very much desire to do anything with my medical degree. Unfortunately I'm not trained to do anything else."

Throughout his presentation, I believed he was speaking directly to me. Everything this doctor was saying rang truer than anything I had heard before in any medical lecture. After only two years in med school, I already felt as dejected and beaten up as this fellow said he was – and I was just getting started. This was the first person in a long time who seemed willing to speak to me honestly and sincerely about my profession, the first to reveal the truth after months of wondering what I had been doing wrong.

His words weren't encouraging, but at least they convinced me that I wasn't crazy, and I wasn't the only one in the room who felt this way.

His story also warned me that I would have to get a lot better at playing the education game, if I were going to survive in this business – *if* I could figure out how to fit into the whole crazy process at all.

Misdirection

Years before entering medical school, I was already practicing the fine art of misdirection. My Junior Magician set came with simple instructions: Hold the big ace up for your audience to see. Move it around a little while you deliver a smooth line of patter, some catchy, meaningless story, laced with a dash of humor. Keep a straight face, maintain eye contact, and no one will notice you slipping the other card out of your pocket with your free hand.

The big surprise was that it worked so well, and so consistently.

The ruse worked well in the hospital, too: Comment on the pretty new floral arrangement, ask about the grandchildren, mention the weather or sports scores or that crazy new TV show while taking a pulse or checking an incision. Find something, anything really, to turn the patients' attention away from their pain and anxiety, some song & dance entertaining enough to distract them during that critical moment when you slip the needle, pull the splinter, remove the dressing. Do it seamlessly, as a regular part of the act, and your audience follows right along. With a little practice, most bedside procedures become painless – for both the patient and the doctor. *Just like magic.*

The versatile magic of misdirection proved to be just as useful during teaching rounds. For some of us, mastering the technique was the key to our academic survival.

Once our training moved out of the classroom and onto the wards, we discovered that the teaching methods changed dramatically. In the lecture hall, the professor's job was to impart medical knowledge to students in a succinct and orderly fashion. If we paid attention and kept up, in all likelihood we would learn enough of the material to get by.

Such was not the case, however, during daily patient rounds. In the halls and at the bedside, we were no longer treated as a group. Here, the goal of the attending physician was to challenge each of us directly, expose our individual ignorance, and humiliate us as thoroughly and as redundantly as possible. This was somehow supposed to encourage us to study harder, presumably to learn enough new material overnight to avoid being embarrassed again the next day:

Attending: "Dr. Jones! Discuss the particulars of the metabolic pathway of arachidonic acid as it relates to the production of prostaglandins and their mediation by non-steroidal anti-inflammatory medications."

"Dr." Jones: (Not really a doctor yet, nonetheless stepping up admirably and clearing her throat like a full-fledged professional) "*Basically*, sir, NSAIDs interfere with prostaglandin production in the tissues."

Attending: "And, assuming by some law of random probability that you may be correct, how do they accomplish this feat of biochemistry?"

Dr. Jones: "By inhibiting the enzyme *cyclo-oxygenase*, which catalyzes *arachidonic acid* to form prostaglandins."

Attending: "And precisely what does that chemical inhibition accomplish in the patient, Dr. Jones?"

Dr. Jones: "Prostaglandins are responsible for establishing the inflammatory response. By disrupting prostaglandin production, NSAIDs reduce pain and swelling in patients."

Attending: "*Pain*, Dr. Jones? What does any of this have to do with pain?"

Dr. Jones: "Uhhh…." She stammers, hugging her clipboard for support.

Attending: "We're *waiting*, Dr. Jones. Don't you think the perception of pain is important to your patient's well being?"

Dr. Jones: "Well, of course… uh… doesn't it have something to do with *bradykinins or something?*"

Attending: "Or *something*. Hmmm. Can anyone else give Dr. Jones a bit of assistance? She seems to be having some difficulty with *pain* just now. Dr. *Smith?*"

Dr. Smith: (With an authoritative tone, a noticeable smirk and a sideward glance at a suddenly deflated Dr. Jones) "Prostaglandins are *also* responsible for producing pain sensations by *directly* stimulating neural membranes. In *addition*, prostaglandins lead to the release of *bradykinin*, which acts on *nociceptors* to amplify pain impulses."

(Whew! Doctor Smith comes through with the correct answer, earning a brownie point for the day, but no brownie. Instead, he suddenly finds his head on the ceremonial chopping block in place of Dr. Jones'.)

Attending: "And just *where* does the arachidonic acid molecule originate to begin the inflammatory cascade?"

Dr. Smith: (Voice cracking, just a little bit) "From somewhere in the damaged cell? The cell membrane?"

Attending: "Are you *telling* me or *asking* me, Dr. Smith? …*Hmph*," he grunts sardonically, pausing for a millisecond before turning to the next victim. "Dr. *Brown?*"

Dr. Brown: "Arachidonic acid is an essential fatty acid component which is released from membrane phospholipids as a response to inflammatory stimuli…"

And so on.

Most of us strove to attain the impossible goal of having an immediate, accurate, and comprehensive answer on hand at all times. We paid attention in lectures. Kept thorough and accurate notes. Stayed up late reading journal papers and medical books. We socialized little, slept less, and stayed constantly, to varying degrees, afraid.

Ostensibly we did this to broaden our understanding of medicine; in fact, we were doing what the professor intended: attempting to avoid daily humiliation by memorizing our textbooks.

We were smart, and we could prove it, but our efforts were never good enough to stand up to the daily challenge. We would never be able to know more than a clinical professor with twenty years' experience. We could never entirely avoid the emotional execution brought on by our necessary ignorance. It surprised me, therefore, that so few of us saw the obvious remedy.

My answer came straight from the Junior Magician kit: keep a straight face, and learn to manipulate the audience. After all, if you're going to get shot down anyway, why not take a bullet voluntarily, then fall out of the line of fire?

It was easy, really. Every day, in preparation for student rounds, I would decide ahead of time just what detail I was going to *forget*. Somehow, inexplicably, some benign factoid regarding one of the patients under my nominal care would simply disappear, *Poof!*

"The sodium level on the patient in 101? Hmmm... Hold on - I know I wrote that down just this morning..." All the while I'm patting my pockets and flipping through note cards as though I'm actually searching for the answer.

The plan was incredibly effective. You could even say it worked like magic.

"Dr. *Stewart*. Would you agree that a patient's *sodium level* is an important value, or are we wasting our time routinely measuring it?"

"Oh, no, it's *important*, sir. Definitely – which is why I'm trying hard to find it. I mean, I should *know* it already, I know, but... wait..."

Of course I knew the patient's sodium level. But if I provided the correct value, promptly and earnestly, I would next be required to produce some other piece of minutia (the exact volume, clarity and coloration of the patient's urine output, for example, or the highest level of a particular liver enzyme that would be considered within normal limits for someone with an obscure tropical disease), the questions becoming more and more abstruse until eventually I would be made to stumble.

That was the whole point of the exercise - to cause me to fail. *To cause each of us to fail*, as often as possible, every day. To remind us at all times that we didn't know enough, *could not ever* know enough to function effectively as practicing physicians. To keep us on the endless treadmill of guilt, guilt, guilt - study, study, study.

Now, I was not at all opposed to the intended outcome of this little game – only the technique. If I did not already have an addictive love of learning, an endless curiosity, and a deep and abiding interest in the study of medicine, I would not have made it this far along the path. None of us would have. In truth I had expected that by this point in our academic careers, that passion would have been recognized and nurtured, encouraged to grow and propagate in a safe, mentoring environment.

I tried to imagine how much more we might have learned – would have *wanted* to learn – had more professors simply commended us when we answered properly, and patiently corrected our mistakes. Instead we were obliged to play The Intimidation Game.

Rather than encourage us through a positive learning experience, The Game depersonalized the process, and dehumanized the players, turning us one against the other in a needlessly competitive melee, every morning at the bedside. The last man standing was somehow superior to his fellows – the better student, the better doctor. King of the Hill – for a day, anyway.

And this was not an empty reward. Long-term success in this artificial competition meant more recognition, higher grades, and glowing recommendations to a superior residency program. Continuing the game led to a staff appointment to some other prestigious teaching facility, where the practice would continue, perpetuating the process of guilt-based learning onto a new generation of medical students. Those who couldn't keep up were destined to wind up interning in out-of-the-way community hospitals, on their way to careers as worker bees in commercial strip-mall clinics. Or so we were told.

Once I became aware of the competition, though, I found I was no longer interested in playing – regardless of eventual reward. Knowing that the game existed at all made me ashamed to be a part of it. So, rather than suffer abuse commensurate with my effort, I simply found it easier to fail early and on purpose, then get out of the way and let someone else take the brunt of the morning ritual. If I died the death of a thousand cuts, no matter. It was going to happen anyway. That was how the game was played.

Yes, I was vaguely aware that my approach would eventually backfire. Like most games, if you don't play, you can't win, and since success in this game was measured by persistence, intentional failure soon registered as ineptitude. Time and again my mentors communicated their disappointment with a word or a gesture, or that off-the-shelf look of sad disapproval. They'd expected so much more from me.

They had no idea how much more I'd expected from them.

Over time, my purposeful lack of participation was replaced by a marked diminution of my interest in the process – or, more truthfully, by the intrusion of other interests. Intentionally or not, my attention was slowly being directed away from medicine, and my life was already being drawn along new lines. I just didn't know it yet.

Appendix

"Dr. *Stew-art!*" Miz Benning hollered down the hall at me from her seat at the nurse's station.

"Yes, Ma'am!" I hollered back, in a manner that anywhere else in the medical center would have been a horrendous breach of protocol. Here at the VA, it was a sign of mutual acceptance, and respect.

"Telephone for you! I'll send it on over to the call room."

"Yes, Ma'am! Thank you!" The phone immediately began ringing in the closet that passed for a resident's lounge. I ran down the hall at full speed to get it – another act that anywhere else in the medical center would have been a horrendous breach of protocol.

"Hello?"

"Hey, there, son, you busy?"

"Not too. What's up?

"Well – I've been spending most of the afternoon lying here on the couch at the office. Can't sit in the chair. I seem to be having a lot of indigestion, and a sore belly."

"What kind of indigestion? What part of your belly hurts? Which end is giving you more trouble? Are you hurting anywhere else?" I was going to have to slow down on the questions, and let him answer one or two of them.

"A little nausea, I guess. Burping, mainly. And my belly sure is sore."

"Upper part or lower part?"

"More like sore all over. I wondered if you'd come take a look at me."

This was new. Dad had never asked me to 'come take a look' at him. Many times he had offered his own opinion about this or that medical condition (he worked for doctors, after all, so he knew what he was talking about), or held forth on the pervasiveness of whining, malingering, laziness in general of people in general, and the wholesale abuse of the medical system by those who could afford to pay for care, but chose not to. Not once had he ever asked my opinion about anything that he hadn't already decided upon himself. And he had never acknowledged any ability on my part for understanding anything about the science or art of medicine. I was still a student. It was my job to learn, not to know.

I consulted with the VA resident who was my boss for this rotation, then ran the five blocks to Dad's office, still wearing the short white coat that identified me and my place in the system. As reported, he was stretched out on the sofa with his tie loosened, his belt undone and his pants unbuttoned. He looked pale.

"How are you feeling?" I asked.

"Not too bad. In fact I think I'm getting a little better." A quick once-over told me he was not doing well at all. His heart and respiration rates were elevated, and he possibly had a mild fever. No one in the office had a thermometer. His skin was clammy, but he had no pain in his chest, back, shoulder or arm. *(It's my stomach that's bothering me, son, not my arm! Weren't you listening?)* He did have generalized lower abdominal tenderness, though, when I pressed gently into his belly, and again when I let go. More alarming, there was no noise in his gut. No rumbles, burbles or tinkles.

Technically speaking, this was *not good.*

I put away my stethoscope.

"I'm actually doing *much* better now," he said, trying to sit up.

"Not so fast," I said. "When was the last time you had a bowel movement?"

"Yesterday morning."

"So you missed today's."

"Come to think of it, I did. But I'm fine."

"What did you have for lunch?"

"Nothing. Didn't feel like it. Had a half a sausage biscuit for breakfast, but I threw that up."

"One last question: What is your favorite food these days? If you had your choice of anything you wanted for dinner, what would it be?"

"I guess it would be spaghetti and meatballs. There's a new restaurant opened a little ways down on highway 280, and..."

"Good. Now imagine, if I brought you a big plate of spaghetti and meatballs right now, would you eat it?"

"Hmm... No, I wouldn't have the appetite for that right now. Maybe later I might..."

"*Pop*," I cut in again. "You're going to the Emergency Room."

"Oh, now don't be *ridiculous*. I just picked up a little bug somewhere, that's all. I'll be alright."

"No, sir, you're *not* alright. You need to see a surgeon. You have a hot appendix, and somebody needs to take a look at it."

"Now son, that's just *crazy*. I told you, I'll be *fine*."

No amount of scolding or cajoling could make him budge. I was still his son, still the student, still lacking the clout that would make him do what he was told. He would rest a while, he said, then head home for a good night's sleep. He'd call me if he needed anything. Thanks for coming over. False alarm.

I spent the rest of the afternoon catching up on rounds, worrying about my father's prognosis. For an insignificant little tag-along with no apparent function, an appendix can sure cause a lot of trouble when it gets disgruntled.

After a few hours I called Dad's house, just to see if he had made good on his word.

"Helloo? Oh, hi… hi, son. Where're you?"

"I'm still at work. Just calling to see how you're doing."

"Oh, I'm doing goood," he slurred. "What're youu up to?"

"*Still at work*. Listen, you don't sound so good. You *sure* you're feeling okay?"

"Yeah. Let me sit up here… been lay-ying back in my chair."

"Pop – you need to come on in to the hospital. We need to check you out."

"No, you don't. I'm fi… Wait a second. There's somebody on the other line…"

"Dad, you don't *have* another line. You're at home."

"No, the red light is blinking here... on the... phone."

"There's no red light on your home phone, Pop. *Now stay there. I'm coming to get you.*"

"No need for that. I can drive myself to the ER."

"*Dad, you don't need to be driving anywhere.* Stay put and I'll come ..."

"I'll just meet you there. I'm fine." He hung up.

I called back, the ancient dial telephone in the VA lounge taking way too long to connect. Dad didn't answer. Either he was already out the door, or sprawled unconscious on the living room floor. I found a phone book and called the neighbors: His car was gone. I thought about calling the police, but decided by the time I got through, he would already be more than halfway to the hospital. Best to run the three blocks to the Emergency room, and inform the nurses *and* the policeman on duty to expect his arrival, either by car or ambulance. God, how I hated being put in these situations. Never a dull moment with Dad.

Fortunately for everybody on the road that night, he managed to pull his massive Lincoln to a stop in the driveway of the ER, and ambled through the automatic sliding doors under his own power. "Go park the car, son," he told me, tossing me his keys.

***

Yes, he appeared to have an *acute abdomen*, an 'operable scenario', the head of Gastro-Intestinal Surgery told me, as my father was being wheeled out of the exam room and up to the OR for a late night appendectomy. No, they would not need my assistance for the procedure. There were residents on call, and a fourth-year student for that. No, I would not be allowed to observe. Didn't I have work to do?

I was only a third-year, after all. A vermiform appendage, not much use to anyone at this stage of my development.

Someone would call me at the VA later that night when he was out of the OR, they said.

No one did.

State of the Art

New Neurosurgery rotation, one a.m. on a Saturday, my first night on call with the brain team. The Knife and Gun Club* were active this evening.

I had just shifted over from Obstetrics a couple of days before, where overnight duty meant being on hand to catch mostly healthy babies emerging from mostly healthy mommies, and retire to the cozy call room as soon as the ordeal was over. Medical students there were scheduled in pairs: I, the wannabe surgeon, woke up only for the Caesarian deliveries; my buddy the aspiring pediatrician gleefully caught all of the babies who came out the way God intended.

Glad to have that experience behind me with but one natural, live birth on my record, I was hoping I could retain just enough of the academic material necessary to pass the obstetrics questions on my general board exams, and leave the rest in my rearview mirror.

Now the excitement of brain surgery was fast replacing a headful of baby facts. Tonight I would see my first craniotomy, my first live brain. I'd have a front row seat to watch these wizards of chirurgy peel back the age-old shrouds of mystery, revealing the source of human thought and action.

We were called to the ER to see an unfortunate 17 year-old urban warrior, caught in the crossfire tonight in a neighborhood confrontation. Emergency X-rays revealed an irregular oval defect in this young man's skull that correlated with the unsightly gap in

*Knife & Gun Club: Victims of violence who arrived in the Emergency Department.

the side of his forehead. The bullet had entered and passed on through, but the damage it had caused was significant. The film also showed a white, triangular fragment of bone lodged deep in the frontal portion of the patient's brain. This would have to come out.

Unresponsive but strong on vital signs, our patient was rushed to the OR to determine the extent of the physical damage to his head, and to see what could be done to save him – or at least salvage as much of 'him' as remained.

The Chief resident filled in a page on the young man's chart with sweeping calligraphy, a pre-operative note cataloguing the surgeon's first impressions in broad strokes from his gold-tipped MontBlanc fountain pen – the anachronistic trademark of our state-of-the-art institution's cutting-edge neurosurgical team.

Patient prepped and intubated, a PGY-3* shaved the area above the wound, and cut a long, semicircular incision through the skin to the bone, all but circumscribing the injury. Bleeding was profuse, and I looked to the Chief to see if he was as alarmed as I was.

"Don't worry," he said. "Heads bleed."

With anticipated precision, the scalp vessels were clamped and cauterized, the skin folded aside, the skull laid bare. Cranial drill in hand, the Chief quickly spun holes through the thin, flat layers of bone, defining the four corners of a squat rectangle. These were cleared of debris with streams of sterile saline solution and a narrow suction device, until a long, thin twist of wire could be passed cleanly beneath the plates of frontal bone.

This wire saw, named for its inventor, Dr. Gigli, evoked an honorary, eponymic chuckle as it was drawn back and forth through the

* Post-Graduate Year 3, a third-year resident

burr holes, cutting the bone from the inside out, angling the edge to a chamfer. Colorful conversation accompanied each step in the process, as late night familiarity replaced the subdued, formal atmosphere of daytime surgery.

The bony plate lifted free to reveal a ragged hole in the dura, a tough layer of tissue that covers the brain like a shower cap. This hole was clogged with a thick mass of clotted blood, rubbery flecks of skin, and tiny shards of bone, mingled with the grey-pink fat of damaged cerebral tissue. The Chief trimmed away the ragged covering, allowing the area beneath to be carefully rinsed and cleaned, with bone, blood and brain matter quickly disappearing down the clear plastic suction tube.

"There. Now we can see what we're working with," he said.

The site looked as though a firecracker had gone off in a bowl of cauliflower pudding. Somewhere in the scrambled void lay a triangular chunk of bone. It was our job to find it.

If this patient had been shot in the arm or leg, the chest or abdomen, our task would have been relatively straightforward: open the area wide, probe deep to locate the offending fragment and pluck it out – rinsing, repairing tissues and closing gaps as we backed our way out of the wound. That works fine when the borders of the damaged area are made of skin, muscle, or viscera. Not so with brain.

In this patient, every bit of surrounding real estate was vital – every cell, every connection constituted the stuff that made this person, *this person*. I was very interested in seeing how trained, state-of-the-art neurosurgeons dealt with this conundrum, removing only the damaged portions, and preserving the precious normal tissue.

Sip, siiip, *slup*! No scissors or scalpels were used to clean up this mess, only sprinkles of water and a rounded metal suction tip.

Tattered bits of grey and white matter disappeared down the tube. Were these memories, I wondered? Feelings? Basic pieces of this young man's personality?

"How can you tell the difference between live brain and dead brain?" I asked, awaiting the first of many glorious neurosurgical revelations that were sure to come. And a revelation it was:

"Dead brain sounds different in the sucker."

Holy *crap*! Surely I hadn't heard that correctly. This guy was kidding. Had to be. This was serious stuff, brain surgery. Chief was obviously making light of a life-and-death situation, putting one over on the new guy. I couldn't see whether he was smiling or frowning behind his surgical mask.

"Seriously, though," I said.

He glanced over at me. It was not a smiling glance.

"See? Listen." He aimed the tip of the suction tube at a piece of greyish material floating in the middle of a blood-tinged pool. *Sloop!* "Now, this," he said, moving the sucker to the edge of the damaged area. *Slooooiiip!*

There was indeed an audible difference. But how much 'good' brain literally went down the tubes before you were sure you heard the right pitch? I guess that's where experience comes in...

"There's no way to tell one hundred percent for sure," Chief went on. "But if we leave any dead tissue in here, it could set this guy up for an infection later on. We take what we have to, spare what we can."

Such was the state-of-the-art in neurosurgery.

My heart fell all the way through my sterile gown to the floor as
the realization sunk in. I continued to watch as fluffy pieces of
brain tissue slipped noisily into the nozzle of the sucker. There
went second grade, for all we knew. There went Aunt Minnie's
lavender-scented, bosomy hug on this guy's tenth birthday. There
went his ability to count change.

"The real question is," Chief continued, "How much are we willing to remove to try and find this one piece of bone?"

It was a dilemma for sure. The half-inch chip had sliced its way
deep into the brain, along a thin, tortuous track, in directions
unknown to us. True, we could see where it ended up on the
X-ray, but we had no way of knowing exactly how it got there.
The Chief was probing blind, with instruments that created an
even wider defect in the tissue, and no real certainty that he was
even heading in the right direction. Bruising and swelling of the
surrounding brain was making the job more difficult with every
passing moment.

"Can't you scan for it?" I asked, in all innocence and sincerity.

A sardonic chuckle rumbled around the operating room.

"Look, it's not like in the movies, kid," said the Chief. "This ain't
Star Trek. We don't have any tri-corders or magic wands in here."

"But they have one upstairs," I offered. No one thought that was
funny.

Neither did I. I mentioned the idea again.

"What the hell are you talking about?" said the Chief.

"Up in the OB ward," I said, drawing on my recent experience in
the birthing room. "They have that new ultrasound machine. The
probe is really small – about the size of your fountain pen."

"And what are we supposed to do with that? This guy doesn't have a baby in his head!"

Hearty laughs all around. This new med student is a riot!

"No, I'm serious! Call up to the OB floor and ask them to bring it down here on the elevator."

"No way. This is a sterile field. See the *brain*? Dumbass."

"So you park the machine in the corner, wrap the wire in sterile towels, and slip the probe into a rubber glove. Then all you have to do is fill up the wound with saline, and drop in the probe. A couple of sweeps and you'll know exactly where the bone fragment is. It'll light up like a Christmas tree!"

I rocked back on my heels, delighted that even as a third year medical student, I had been able to contribute directly to the care of a patient. This new approach would save time and effort, and would minimize the amount of cutting required to remove that piece of bone. Less trauma, less risk of infection. It might even lower the risk of this man having seizures in the future. There was no way this wasn't a terrific idea. We could even write a paper about it...

"You done?" said the Chief. The rest of the team continued to stifle their laughter.

"Sure. Do you want me to break scrub, and go get the equipment from upstairs?

"What I want you to do is be quiet, and quit distracting me. We're here to operate. You're here to shut the hell up and learn."
So I was.

I watched the rest of the procedure in silence. Chief probed a while longer before deciding to abandon the search for the missing bone. He closed the wound, and sent his patient to Intensive Care. "We'll cover him with antibiotics," Chief said.

The next day I asked one of the other residents why my idea had been dismissed. Turns out that medicine is a risk-averse business. (*No kidding.*) In a teaching hospital, we learn how things *are* done, not how they *might* be done. (*Why not learn both?*) You don't get rewarded for straying outside of the box.

"Nobody cares what medical students think. Remember that. Your job is to do as you're told," I was told. "Keep your nose clean, and if you last long enough, maybe one day you'll get to try out some of your cock-eyed ideas. Until then, keep your mouth shut."

Little chance of that happening, I thought.

Graduation

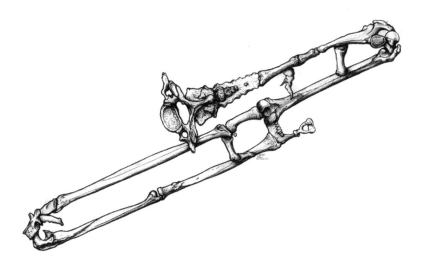

Authority Issues

"You have *authority issues*, don't you?" he told me, anticipating my agreement.

She hugged herself a little tighter then, fists clenched, eyes narrowed, her thin arms crossed at once in pitiable self-defense and righteous defiance: A shot landed, a point scored. That'll show me.

We had started these sessions sitting together on the couch. Now, five weeks later, we sat in separate chairs in front of the counselor's desk. She shifted in her seat, pulling herself another half inch away from me.

"I suppose I do, but I don't see how that figures into this situation."

"You don't like to be told what to do. Isn't that right?"

"I don't know anyone who does. Not unless there's a good reason."

"But that's the whole point, don't you see? Sometimes we have to do what we're told, without knowing the reason. Can you understand that?"

"I understand that you're speaking to me as though I were a child. I *don't* understand *that*."

He churched his fingers, resting his lower lip on the steeple.

"Let's start over. You came in to see me because your marital relationship was in trouble. I'm telling you how you can go about fixing it. Now you don't like hearing what I am telling you, and you are putting up resistance. That's not at all good for your marriage."

The counselor was a little off his game today. If this was meant to be a curve ball, it was coming in awfully straight.

"On the contrary," I said, "We came to see you because I felt our *pre*-marital relationship did not seem strong enough to support a healthy marriage. If anything, you have confirmed that suspicion. By following your instructions, pretending to be happy in an unhappy situation, I feel we would only be putting off the inevitable."

"So you've given up? You've decided to stop trying?"

Her face began to pale.

"Given up? Not at all. I have decided to stop *lying*." That should do it. Brace for impact.

"So you *admit* that you haven't been truthful. That you've been lying to us."

Duck. Dodge. Parry:

"Not intentionally. Mostly I've been lying to myself. We came here for answers, and I believe we have found them. Now I'm finding it harder and harder to keep fooling myself, believing that everything is okay."

"So now you want to try and improve your relationship by ignoring my advice. You know, Don, you can't go through life asking for help, and then rejecting it. You'll never get anywhere like that." Zing. "Unless you agree to change, you can never expect to grow as an individual."

Wow. A twofer.

"Oh, I agree to change alright." Up went the eyebrows. His, this time. Not mine.

"Do you? Tell me, then, how do you see yourself in the future, if you aren't willing to take direction? Where will you be a year from now? Ten years from now?"

"Again, I don't believe that I am unwilling to take direction, so long as there is a clear benefit to everyone involved. I just don't see the wisdom of following a particular path without knowing why. Especially if that path is taking me in a direction I don't want to go."

At this point his disappointment in me began to slip, slowly but perceptibly, into disdain. His curdled expression telegraphed a growing sense of personal failure: mine, for refusing to accept his version of my adult responsibility; his, for not convincing me to do so.

As his mood noticeably dimmed the room, her eyes brightened. This was what she had been hoping for in today's engagement: a flicker of open conflict, the kind she seemed to thrive on. Only I didn't feel like playing this game any longer.

"But to answer your question, where will I be a year from now? In a residency program somewhere up north, holding retractors and working my ass off. Following directions, no doubt."

He flashed to anger at the last part, but controlled it, waiting to see whether or not I was intentionally baiting him. I wasn't. Not then, not ever.

I had wanted to approach my first experiment in counseling with a clean slate, an open heart, and no agenda other than to answer the question at hand: *Do we really want to go through with this?* I was looking forward to it, mostly, but knew there would be problems – problems to be worked out, and problems with the process.

During my training, the psych professors told me that one of the biggest challenges to therapy was uncovering the hidden agendas. You have to deal with those, they said, before you can ever get to the real issues.

They didn't tell me that the counselor would be working out his agenda, too.

The fact that I had worked with him up to this point should have shown that I was open to the process, but by now I was really starting to question the need to put up with any more of his questionable technique. After surviving decades of emotional manipulation at home, this marriage was supposed to be the start of a forty-year exercise in honesty and mutual support, a happy journey toward common goals.

But today's proceedings were starting to take on a familiar aroma.

Prior to these five sessions of premarital introspection, she and I had each undergone extensive background interviews, read pamphlets on the Responsibilities of Marriage, and filled out detailed personality assessments. We were even required at one point to draw out our families' divorce pedigrees – family trees showing failed marriages for as far back as either of us was aware. Each of these exercises proved to be informative, and enlightening.

"Hmmm… That's funny. None of these answers matches the question they're asking here."

"Hush! We're *not supposed to talk* while we're taking the test!"

"I'm not asking for help. I'm just saying that sometimes none of the multiple choice answers they give fit the questions."

"Just mark down the closest one."

"There's *not* a closest one. I'm just going to leave this one blank."

"*You* can't *leave it blank!*" she hissed. "The instructions say to answer every one. *Every. One.* If you don't answer it, they won't be able to tell whatever they're trying to find out about you."

"I imagine it will tell them more about me than if I put down an answer that isn't true. Take this question up here, for instance… this one has *two* good answers. So I marked them both."

"You can't *do* that! You're only allowed to pick *one* answer. They *said: One* answer *per* question."

"They also said to answer each question honestly," I emphatted. "That's what I'm doing."

"They're just going to mark it wrong. Those are the rules."

Rules were important to her, and the tests confirmed it. For me, not so much. I might need guidance, but more important, I needed purpose. I could work endlessly for a cause I believed in, and be happy with the effort. She would work because she was supposed to, then nurture her righteous resentment forever afterward.

Our test results reflected a similar string of polarities. The four-letter personality types assigned to us shared no common characters. In conversation she said she preferred quiet time alone at home; her tests revealed a strong tendency to seek external fulfillment. I was just the opposite: outgoing in appearance, but on closer inspection quite happy keeping my own company.

The marriage counselor was delighted with these results. He determined that in our differences, we represented the *perfect match,* each of our individual strengths and weaknesses counteracting and balancing the other. *Interdigitating* was the word he used, lacing his fingers together in front of us to demonstrate the strength of this special bond. "See? It's *watertight!*"

His professional enthusiasm aside, it was the pedigrees that finally convinced me otherwise.

The pictures staring back at us from the blackboard in his office could not have been more disparate. She was able to accurately depict, from memory, her family relations back through four generations on one side, five on the other. There were no divorces, ever. *None*, unless you count the one great uncle whose first wife was institutionalized back in the forties for schizophrenia. No, wait - she killed herself in the hospital before he remarried. So, *None*.

"Once The Lord has joined two people together, it's a *sin* to get a divorce," she said more than once, with grave and righteous finality. Her people weren't always happy, but they stayed together, by God. Come Hell or high water.

In glaring contrast, my family tree barely made its way through three widely spread generational branches before its limbs became hopelessly disfigured by a procession of failed unions. Just considering my parents, aunts, uncles, and first cousins, the body count was already in the double digits. We were a passionate family, for sure – quick to love, but not too keen on suffering needlessly. My great grandmother may have gone to her grave uncertain of her Heavenly reward, but she was satisfied that when her husband rose up to beat her on this Earthly plane, she put him out of her house at knifepoint.

When the going got tough in our family, the tough ones held their ground. It was their partners who got going.

How did I explain this tragic, repetitive trend in my family's history? Well, by all accounts our people were known to be opinionated and stubborn, and quick to defend whatever they believed in. My guess was, too, that the kinfolk following their hearts into high holy matrimony probably didn't do enough head work on the front end.

I was afraid we hadn't done enough of it, either. These counseling sessions confirmed my suspicions.

"He just wants me to be his mother," she lobbed.

"How do you respond to that, Don?" the counselor said, giving me the chance to step up and take the hit.

"She has a valid point. There's a lifetime of nurturing I missed out on, because of my mother's death, because I was so young at the time. I am certainly eager to take every chance I can get to make up for the intimacy I never experienced growing up."

He nodded, knowingly.

"But does that mean that I am somehow imposing upon her in this relationship? Maybe, if she's not comfortable being intimate with me."

"You know you can't expect her to replace your mother."

"And she knows that I've never asked her to. I don't need a mother. I do need to be understood and appreciated emotionally, and physically. I thought that was what marriage was all about. Perhaps we could try and understand why that is so difficult for her to do?"

"We were talking about you."

"We seem to be doing that a lot."

I said that I needed love, and acceptance, and sex. She said that she wanted to be married, and maybe she wanted to have children, too. She reaffirmed her willingness to accept all the responsibilities, burdens and social rewards pertaining to each of those decisions. (What became less and less clear as the meetings wore on, was whether she wanted at all to be married to *me*.)

That was it, in a nutshell, the marriage counselor said. *She* was acting responsibly. *I* was acting emotionally. He was right, of course. She was ready to "commit" herself to a well-defined role. Forever. I was "feeling" perplexed, and neglected, and alone. Not the sort of "feelings" one ought, I "felt", to associate with impending marriage. Definitely not the way I wanted to "feel" for the next four decades.

Nonsense, said the counselor. The key problem in our relationship had been identified, and it was *me*. I was unwilling to submit to the counselor's authority, or to authority in general, and was therefore unable to make the concessions that would be necessary to maintain a healthy, mature union. I should be ashamed of myself. I should be more responsible.

She sat with her hands in her lap, twirling the diamond engagement ring on her finger, waiting for me to respond. Whether she agreed with him completely, or was merely giving me the chance to protest and ratchet the drama up another notch, I couldn't tell.

"Explain not," I heard my Grandmother say, somewhere deep in the back of my mind. *"Your friends don't require it, and your enemies won't believe you, anyway."*

Suddenly I found myself marveling, terrified actually, at the thought that in his mind and hers as well, avoiding shame and acting responsibly *were the same thing.* Then I realized that this was exactly how I had been raised: shamed into doing what others told me I was supposed to do. Forced to do what others expected of me, for no other reason than it *was* expected. Pressed into a mold that didn't fit.

Just like this one.

"Let's say you're right," I continued. "I could behave myself. I could yield to your authority, and to her expectations, and take it on faith that everything will be a-okay. But then I'd still have to deal with the *feeling* that we're all on the wrong track, and about to crash."

"You need to learn not to rely so much on your imagination."

"Yeah, but when this whole thing falls apart, who's going to take responsibility for *that*?"

"It's your job to make sure *that* doesn't happen." He chided, glad to finally be making some headway with me. "With her help, of course. You two are a team, you know." He held up two fingers, pressed together, to illustrate his point.

"Maybe, but I feel like I'm missing the ol' team spirit. And this time I'm afraid I'm going to have to pay attention to that feeling."

He stared at me accusingly from across the desk, his two fingers still pressed together, only now they were aiming at the middle of my chest. She stared at me accusingly from her chair.

"What's *that* supposed to mean?" they asked, in unison.

"What it *means* is," I said, turning to my betrothed, "A year from now, there is very little chance that you and I are going to be a couple. These sessions have convinced me of that."

"But we have *plans*..." she began.

"We *both* have plans. Unfortunately your plans for our future are a whole lot different than mine."

"*But the wedding!*"

"Oh, we can go through all the motions. If you want to, we can have a great big wedding, and a honeymoon. We can even move all our stuff together into a single household.

But the operative word here is *single*. Whatever we do, in spite of or even because of our best efforts, I'm pretty sure that by this time next year, I'll be on my own again."

Expensive Care Unit

The man had nine tubes connected to his body on the day he died.

Two IVs directed fluids and medications, drugs flowing into one arm to keep his blood pressure up, in the other to coax the pressure back down, with antibiotics, anti-emetics, acid blockers, blood thinners and pain killers piggy-backed onto Y-shaped access ports, or pumped in measured doses through blue computerized boxes clamped to shiny metal IV poles.

A third line penetrated deep into the man's chest, entering above the his collar bone, coursing through the great thoracic vessels and the right-side chambers of his heart, its round balloon tip resting snugly in the terminal arteries of his lungs. Above, a thin yellow feeding tube emerged spaghetti-like from his nose, while down below a thick red rubber catheter drained the man's bladder into a bag hooked onto the side of his bed. Another did what it could to channel the volumes of liquid feces that had plagued this patient for too many days, and took up far too much of the intensive care nurses' valuable time in sanitary maintenance, skin care and linen changes.

Clear plastic tubes the size of small garden hoses exited either side of the patient's chest, each connected to a low-suction vacuum canister that functioned to keep his fragile lungs inflated – lungs that had already popped like loose bubble-wrap from the air forced into them through a similar tube that traversed the length of his throat. This was the tube he had hoped to avoid. The one that just one week earlier he made me promise, *promise* not to let anyone put into him.

That tube was the one that caused all the trouble.

My patient knew it would, the day he entered the hospital.

I was in my last month of medical school, on call during my senior Internal Medicine rotation. Our attending physician was away at a medical conference; the responsibility for daily patient care decisions fell on the shoulders of residents and interns. Because of time constraints and the trickle-down process of medical education, some of the grown-up work landed in the hands of medical students like me.

My patient was a 56-year-old emaciated white male, desperately short of breath, with the purple cheeks and blue lips characteristic of end-stage emphysema, the result of decades of cigarette smoking. I asked him how long he had smoked, how any packs per day, then calculated his addiction in pack-years and recorded the number in his Social History.

"I'm not long for this world, Doc, and I know it," he said to me matter-of-factly, pausing to take a labored breath. "I been in and out of hospitals for a while now, and I know my time's a-comin'... What I want to know is whether you can do anything for me this time... That's all... Talk straight to me, Doc. I can handle it... If there's a few more good days left for me, I'll take 'em... I don't expect much more out of life, but if you can get me breathin' again,... good enough to take the grandkids out fishin' another time or two, I'd be grateful... If you can't, I just want you to send me on home."

A review of his hospital chart told me that my patient had a clear grasp of his medical condition, and his likely prognosis. He had been breathing from an oxygen tank at home for a number of years. He was taking maximum doses of stimulants and bronchodilators, and had suffered multiple bouts of pulmonary infections requiring multiple hospital admissions, and escalating rounds of antibiotics – each infection destroying more and more of his precious lung tissue.

"One thing you've got to promise me, Doc," he said. "You can't put me on a breathing machine... I don't want no tubes in my throat. Don't want to die that way. *Promise me.*"

I assured him that his wishes would be followed to the letter, and dutifully transcribed his directive onto his chart: *Do Not Intubate. Do Not Resuscitate.* In the meantime, I ordered laboratory tests, chest x-ray, and breathing treatments that would hopefully provide the "tune up" he needed to return home for his last days.

After a weekend in the hospital my patient was breathing more easily, and was more relaxed when our Attending returned on Monday to make his morning rounds. The boss was encouraged by our patient's progress, but was concerned that the man was still having a hard time getting enough air.

"We need to rest your chest muscles," the doctor said. "I think you would do well to spend a day or two letting a machine do your breathing for you."

The man shot a panicked look my way. "Doctor," I began. "This patient has requested that he not be placed on a ventilator..."

Immediately I was taken by the elbow and ushered away from the bedside, out into the hallway. My resident whispered: "On this service, you don't speak unless you are spoken to. *Understand?*"

"But we had this conversation when I admitted him. He *specifically* denied intubation! It's right there on his *chart!*"

"Doesn't matter. He's not your patient."

I was not allowed to speak of it again. The man who was not my patient trusted all of his doctors, and eventually consented to a few days of artificial respiration, to 'rest his breathing muscles'. After that, he could go home.

But things did not go as planned. Things, in fact, did not go well at all. Rather than improve on the ventilator, the man's condition deteriorated rapidly. Within hours, his oxygen fell to critical levels. We transferred him at once to the Intensive Care Unit.

"We need to get that tube out of him," I said.

"Nonsense," the resident retorted. "That tube is keeping him alive."

"But what if he doesn't want to *be* alive?"

In the ICU, our patient managed to pull the breathing tube from his throat not once, but twice, forcing the staff to restrain him, tying his hands to the sides of the bed.

"Take this thing out!" he mouthed silently, over and over again, gesturing angrily at the tube, the damned tube that prevented him from voicing his desire to be left alone, to be sent home, that kept him from cursing at us with what shallow remnants of vigor and determination that he had left.

"How can we do this?" I asked my resident, again and again. "How can we continue to ignore this man's distress, and his obvious, express desire for us to *stop*?"

She explained it all to me once more, her patience waning, her own discomfort with the system, and her place in it, beginning to show through.

This patient had been placed on low-dose morphine, she said, as prophylaxis against the discomfort and anxiety of being intubated. That was standard procedure. Being hooked to a breathing machine is irritating at best. Lying immobilized in an intensive care bed, unable to speak or even sleep with needles sticking into your skin, nurses bothering you around the clock, and the constant buzz and beep of medical monitoring equipment can be terrifying. Hence the morphine.

The tragic implication for the patient was this: the medication also took away his right to choose.

Since morphine acts on the brain, it alters the patient's mental state, and renders him incompetent from a legal standpoint. It no longer mattered what he said, or how vehemently he communicated to us that we stop his treatment. We were obliged by law and the code of ethical conduct to ignore his pleas.

The last morning I saw my patient, the man I could not help, this suffering human being I was *not allowed* to help, I found a hand-written note clipped to the front of the chart, the words scrawled in a shaky hand across the page. The nurses had responded to his pantomimed request for a pen and pad, and had held the clipboard for him while he jotted down his message.

"I'm sorry," he wrote. "I don't mean to be a bad patient."

He died thinking all of this was his fault.

Within hours the air pressure from the ventilator popped his left lung like a thin balloon, then his right. A day later his kidneys stopped working, and his liver began to fail.

Soon after, his circulation became erratic, his heart gave up, and the man who was not my patient was dead. So was any desire I ever had to be a part of a system that could work so diligently to torment a human being this way, and believe it was right in doing so.

Weeks later I accepted my medical degree, knowing that my life's calling had in fact been a tragic error. I recited the Hippocratic oath with the heavy heart of a well-intentioned fraud.

I still had five years of surgical training ahead of me, and after that the challenge of building my own practice, in an industry I had already come to despise. I was stuck on the assembly line, with no room for complaint, and no clear avenue of escape.

I Have No Idea

She lay obtunded in her hospital bed, at the end of the step-down ward adjacent to Intensive Care. I don't remember what her initial complaint had been, or what had happened to her since she arrived. Whatever had brought her to the hospital, what course that disease had taken, which complications of what treatment had manifested themselves in that day's clinical presentation have long since bled from my memory.

She was relatively young, dark-complected, obese. No longer intubated, I remember that.

And she was sleepy, just this side of comatose. She had been worked up every which way for infections, circulation problems, central nervous system disorders, metabolic & endocrine diseases, and a whole herd of zebras*. We were now looking at pharmaceutical interactions – side effects caused by the daily cocktail of drugs we had been pumping into her unresponsive body.

"Dr. Stewart, which of our patient's medications might account for her current clinical state?"

I thought about it for a second, mentally reviewing the list of drugs she was taking, trying to recall their individual actions, side effects, interactions… I hadn't made it very far down the list before my train of thought jumped the track, plummeted into a dark ravine and began piling up onto itself. I considered sending in recovery teams, looking for survivors, but decided instead to go back to the station, and start again.

*Zebra: A rare condition. When you hear hoof beats drumming outside in the street, what animal is making the noise? Sure, it *could* be a zebra, or some guy playing with a pair of coconut shells. Most likely, though, it's a horse.

"Well?" the Attending prodded.

This time my mind went utterly blank, an impenetrable cloud of fatigue and defeat.

"I have no idea," I said, acknowledging the simple truth.

"What the hell kind of answer is that?" the doctor shot back.

"An honest one, I'm afraid."

The rest of the team sucked in their breath.

"*And that's good enough for you?*" he barked. "Here you are, what, less than a month – what is it – *two weeks* away from graduation, and that's the best you can come up with? *'I have no idea?'* Where are you going to be six months from now, *Doctor*, when you have your degree, and your own patients to take care of? When you're the one they're relying on to come up with the right diagnosis? "

"No one is more concerned about that than I am, sir, but it doesn't change the fact that right now I don't know the answer to your question."

One student gasped. The other members of the team stood wide-eyed and open-mouthed.

"Hell, Doctor! Right now it doesn't sound very much like you care at all!"

He was right. Just then, I didn't care. At all.

Sure, I was concerned about the patient and her condition. I wished her well. I wished desperately that I could *make* her well. But it was clear that my success or failure in answering this question was not going to make a bit of difference to this girl.

111

Under the close supervision of multiple staff docs, residents and students from a half dozen different consulting services, and three shifts of ex-pert nurses, this lady was going to get better or worse without my intervention. At that moment there was nothing I could do to influence her prognosis one way or another.

And that didn't bother me one damn bit.

A Perfect Opportunity

God missed the perfect opportunity to take me Home that night.

I told Him so right there, right out loud, staring up at the cloud-less sky from a field by the side of the road, as the last of the gasoline trickled out onto the pavement from my folded, rup-tured tank.

Midnight, a month before medical school graduation: Foot on the brake, idling at a stoplight on a county road somewhere east of the city, I reached down to change the cartridge in my state-of-the-art Quadrophonic 8-track tape player, standard equipment in this new-to-me Buick Riviera, tricked out with velour bucket seats, moon roof, padded Landau top and designer trim – and a not-at-all standard turbocharged V-8 engine. The night was quiet beyond the hum of our motors, and would have been velvet dark without the mercury lamps flooding the parking lot over at the corner store. We'd be at the lake in half an hour.

I had never been bitten by the auto bug before. Before my Riv-iera, cars were a hand-me-down convenience, a cheap, reliable method of getting from here to there, and hopefully back again. Make, model, and horsepower meant absolutely nothing.

If the engine ran and the pedals worked, I was happy. If the car looked good too, well, that was a bonus.

This car, though – *this* car was different. This car found *me*. Something about the vehicle reached out from the side of the highway, called to me from the gravel lot where in other seasons men peddled loads of firewood or pine straw or watermelon or tomatoes from the backs of rusted pickup trucks.

Oh, yes – it beckoned. This car wanted to run its last laps with me behind the wheel.

There were no rusted trucks that day. Just one flawless cream-colored sedan, sparkling in the dappled sunlight, taunting me with a fresh coat of polish and gleaming wire wheels, trumpeting its availability with a large, neon-red FOR SALE sign in the window.

I didn't have to write down the number. It stuck day-glo in my mind all the way home, stayed there while I picked up the phone and dialed the proud, despairing owner. He hated to get rid of it, he said, this young man who suddenly found himself between jobs, with a new wife and a baby on the way. It was gonna hurt for sure, but what could he do? Glad to help, I told him, handing over the full balance in my bank account the very next day, all in a single check.

This would be money well spent, I told myself. In a few more weeks I would be driving a thousand miles north to begin my residency. I would need a good car to get me there, and the reliability of front-wheel drive to carry this Southern boy through the legendary depths of a snow-packed Midwestern winter. No, this wasn't a matter of desire at all. It was a question of safety. I *needed* this car.

Back then, Buick was not known for producing high-performance automobiles. Big as a full-sized family car, their Riviera model defined the structural limits of the two-door land yacht. More stylish than the rest of their blue-hair-friendly line, this was the affordable, middle-class version of Cadillac's Eldorado, a disco-era favorite of budget- and image-conscious bachelors with things to see and people to do.

A huge V-8 engine delivered enough power to move the Riviera's massive frame nimbly through traffic, and still achieve impressive speeds on the open road. And with a full-fledged turbocharger

Frankensteined under the hood, this car could instantly turn any stretch of interstate into a raceway.

Once I tested the engine's capacity to run wide open, late at night on a new ten-mile stretch of bypass, a section not yet opened to regular traffic. Slipping around the construction barricades, I found the middle of an unpainted three-lane highway, slid back the moon roof and punched the accelerator. Tiny indicator lights on the dashboard flashed from green to yellow to red, as the turbocharger engaged, spun up, and achieved maximum rpm. In smooth response, the engine gave a low, throaty growl, woofed into overdrive, and shot down the interstate, reaching 110 mph without straining a muscle. Wind whistling through the open top turned the inside of the car into a vortex, loud enough to drown out Phil Collins' *Take... Take Me Home* on the 8-track system. I finally let up when the speedometer pegged above 120, then coasted back to 50 before the next exit ramp widened off to the right.

Now that I knew what a real car could do, I never again had the desire to drive beyond the limits. Once was enough. With this car, it would have to be. I would be taking no more chances with my new machine.

I spent my spare time that early spring cleaning and polishing the chrome, replacing the vinyl on the padded roof, restoring the Buick to its original factory glow. This was my therapy and my delight, and a welcome distraction from the uncertainties and disappointments that plagued me through my final days of medical school. Maybe I couldn't save people, but I could certainly bring this car back to life.

What I could not complete on my own, I turned over to the professionals: Complete tune-up by a bona-fide racing mechanic. New opera lamps. Factory floor pads. Touch-up paint with hand-run pinstripes. Fully detailed, inside and out - even the new whitewall tires were cleaned and polished to a deep ebony glow. They discharged my Riviera from the body shop show-room new, less than eight hours before the accident.

***

Back at the intersection, a new day was ticking forward on my in-dash digital chronometer. Finally off of the call schedule and away from the hospital, I was heading out of town for a quiet weekend of fishing at a friend's family cabin, his well-worn Chevy Nova leading the way out to the country. Now it was rumbling low, idling impatiently between the red light and my Riv.

I leaned down to change the cartridge in the tape player, plugging in Billy Joel's 'Innocent Man', sliding it home with a flick of an index finger. *That's interesting,* I thought to myself, as the car suddenly, silently filled with light. *This tape player must be wired in to the dome... How is that poss...*

Then came the push, the big bear hug, my older brother jumping out from some hiding place in the back seat and grabbing me from behind. *No, that's not him.* This was the bucket seat, cradling me, wrapping me on three sides in deep plush velour foam, expelling an audible *koosh* of air, still fragrant from a fresh shampoo.

Just then a handful of rice floated against the back of my head, tunneling its way deep into my hair. *Like a wedding,* I thought. *Yeah, like a wedding,* I imagined again, as tiny, barley-bits of glass tumbled past my ears, showering the control panel, bouncing and twirling in the light like diamonds...

Oh, Crap! And the lights were gone, snuffed out by the sound of two refrigerator-sized, double-thick corrugated boxes crumping and folding one into the other – not a *crash* at all, but a deep, muffled *WHUMF!* that shuddered through the vehicle and held me upright, buried in the cushioning depths of the driver's seat. For a splinter of a second I heard glass pebbles dance slow motion along the dash, drawing my attention to the car ahead. The Nova was expanding, rapidly, filling the movie screen of my windshield with horizontal bars of shining silver and rusted navy blue.

My foot automatically pushed harder on the brake pedal, as my own headlights grew day-bright against the flashing chrome of the Nova's rear bumper. I shut my eyes before the second *WHUMF!* shot me face-first toward the steering wheel. *Brace for impact!* I thought. *Too late for that!* I answered back, or would have, given even a sliver of normal time. The seatbelt and shoulder harness tightened around my hips and chest, almost soon enough to prevent contact. I kissed the wheel roughly (*How can I be this close?*), hard enough to earn a fat lip and bloody nose, then glanced up to see the Nova rocket forward and shrink through the intersection, bouncing its flat, shiny tail up and down on wide, slick racing tires.

***

Okay, I'm awake.

My car is still, and quiet, and dark. My ears are ringing. The traffic light overhead is changing from green, to yellow, to red. Billy Joel has stopped singing. (Did he ever start?) My seat has shifted all the way forward, and then some — the front of my jacket is brushing up against the steering wheel...

Do a quick systems check. Hands, feet: fine. Head: good. Nose, a little thick. Sniff test: Yep, a misty taste of blood. I'm all right.

The car is not.

A quick look tells me that the front passenger's seat is stuffed all the way under the dash. The trunk lid is Z-folded back onto itself, reaching through the rear window and over the back seat like a ragged hand, its pointed fingers hovering inches from my right temple. Pebbled safety glass is everywhere.

Out of the silence, I hear the sound of water running from the rear of the vehicle, a lavatory tap turned full on. *Can't be the radiator. What's left of that is still somewhere in front of me... Nope, not raining, it's a clear night... so what could be... Oh... SHIT!*

I reached over, then back for the door handle, reminding myself not to panic. The latch clicked, but the long door wouldn't budge, pinned in place by a bent front quarter panel. I unsnapped the shoulder harness and gave the door another hard shove, concentrating my strength against the sound of grating metal. It moved, a little – enough to squeeze my head through, then my shoulders, hips, and legs, one at a time. I stumbled backwards out of the wreck, hopping on one foot to keep from falling.

The sound of splashing water was louder outside of the car, the bright smell of high-octane gasoline rising up from the pavement near my feet. Time to walk. Walk away. *Fast.*

An old Bobby Sherman tune popped unbidden into my head. *Easy come, and easy go.* So this is what he was singing about. My car, my life... *Easy come, easy go.*

Men came running toward me from the left and right. "You alright?" they were calling. "Yeah, I think so." I smiled awkwardly at myself, shrugged, even laughed a little at the absurdity of the situation. "Easy come, easy go."

They exchanged glances among themselves, then suggested that I come over and sit down under the light. The cops and firefighters were on their way.

My friend was fine. So, astonishingly, was the guy who hit me. On his way home from night school after studying late, he was working overtime to finally earn a degree, years later than he expected.

"Don't know how I could have hit you," he said. "I saw you from

a half a mile back, easy. Saw you stopped at the light, thought I
was slowing down."

Instead he had fallen fast asleep, hit the gas, and hit me dead-on
at sixty miles an hour.

His miniature pickup truck was totaled. No, no one knew how
he would be able to afford another one. He spent the next hour
sliding back and forth between despair and elation: His truck was
gone, but he was alive – and I was alive. How glad he was that I
was alive.

No damage done to the Nova. None! God, those things are
tough. A solid anvil, that car. Cast iron. Who cares if they get five
miles to the gallon.

My car was dead at the scene, naturally: the crumpled husk of
a dream, wadded up like a Polaroid photo of an old girlfriend.
"Nope, that one's gone for sure," the bystanders murmured to
themselves, to each other. "That's a real shame." "No fixing that."
"Pretty car, too."

I wondered how so many people could wind up hanging out at a
Seven-Eleven, at one in the morning, out here in the middle of
nowhere.

A tow truck would arrive soon, chirping reverse toward the front
of my wreck. Its driver would get out and puzzle over the remains, wondering just where he would be able to fix his cables.
He'd know nothing of my loss – his job would be to haul away
the trash, file the paperwork, and maybe get an hour or two of
sleep before breakfast.

Reviewing the wreckage the next day, an insurance adjustor would
wonder out loud how anyone could have escaped this Riviera
alive at all, much less unharmed. He'd point with the back end of
his ballpoint pen, then write on his clip board:

Radiator wrapped around the engine block.
Engine flattened against the firewall.
Back seat folded forward, displaced by the contents of what
used to be the trunk...

He would point out how all of the seats had been sheared from the floorboard. "Hell, the only thing holding that one in place is the safety belt!"

There would in fact be just enough room among the folds of metal and upholstery for one human being, the one in the driver's seat.

While firemen finished hosing down the pavement with water and flame retardant foam, I wandered through the pasture next to the highway, fists punched deep into my jacket pockets, and looked up at the stars.

"You missed Your chance to take me back", I told The Almighty, shoulders squared, jaw set, talking straight to His face. "You'd better have something good waiting for me there up north," I dared Him. "'Cause around here, things pretty much suck."

***

I have not come close to communicating the simple things that I wanted to say in this piece:

I was in love with my car.
It was fun. It was thrilling. It responded as promised.

While the rest of my life was runneling into the sewer in a river of pus and mucus and rejection and failure and dashed expectations all around, my car was the one thing that I could count on to bring me pleasure.

It was powerful. Attractive. Reliable.

I was impotent, ugly, and lost.

According to society I should have been on top of the world, looking forward to the next phase of my training, one step closer to a rewarding, prestigious career. Instead I was glad to have medical school all but behind me, shaken off like the last phlegmatic cough of a lingering pox.

In the last four years I had learned that the Ivory Tower was a whitewash. That lives were less important than legalisms. The humorous line between Hippocratic and hypocrite-ic wasn't funny any more.

But, I had my car – and in it the outward and visible signs of what I hoped my life would one day offer: Strength. Beauty. Style. Quiet power. Some small measure of distinction. Then, just as this dismal chapter of my life was drawing to a blessed close, my car was gone, too. Just. Like. That.

I felt like nothing that night. I felt numb. I felt cheap and empty and worthless as a fragment of a ruptured balloon. I felt like I had been cheated, again, by God, by Fate, by everything but the physics of momentum and metallurgy – my dying dreams tied up in the metaphor of an automobile's demise.

Was I suicidal before the wreck? Afterwards? No. The psychometrists were still wrong on that score. I'll admit that I was more than a little disappointed with Death, though. He truly had not been paying close enough attention to his work that evening.

But I did stand outside and declare to the sky that a colossal error had been made, an opportunity missed to take me Away. Surely after the wreck there was nothing left for me here, and yet here I stood.

You'd better have a plan, I told Him.

'Cause I was *done.*

Internship

Marketable Skills

As pre-meds, medical students and residents, we were trained to digest information in huge quantities, make it our own, and then act upon it, appropriately, in the shortest possible time. We read volumes of new material on a daily basis, wrote reams of notes in classrooms and laboratories, filled patient charts with observations, evaluations and treatment plans, edited endlessly for presentations and scholarly journals. We managed Sisyphean work schedules, juggled clinical information, lab data, meds, specimens, x-rays, and patient progress around the clock, for days on end, with other people's lives and our own sanity hanging in (at times, it seemed, *sliding off*) the balance.

We learned to interact meaningfully with people from all walks of life, complete strangers from every stratum of society, representing every facet of intelligence, education, opinion and belief, to ferret out the most intimate and critical information – all in a matter of minutes. Not only did this process teach us how to be good doctors, it forced us to be good time and resource managers. In addition, it qualified us to be excellent writers and editors, investigative reporters, researchers, detectives, actors, salesmen, social workers, teachers, business administrators, civic leaders, babysitters, and, for those of us who were paying attention, comedians of the highest order.

The O.R. is a tough room to play, though, especially for an intern. I soon discovered that a sense of humor was more appreciated by my patients than by the surgical staff, who seemed to equate a serious demeanor and stern countenance with dedication to the job. But my bedside manner demanded a good exit line; I did my best to leave them laughing whenever appropriate, and that was most of the time. Humor was a time-tested physic, with a low incidence of negative side effects. At the very least I found that a kind and earnest word, and a genuine smile would often serve to lift the burden of pain and hopelessness and fear from my patients and their families.

I also found that a decent academic track record, personable demeanor, above-average manual skills, and an intense desire to learn the secrets of surgical intervention were no match for the competitive environment of a pyramid training program.

Most surgical residency programs are based on the Pyramid System, an academic Ponzi scheme with lots of first- and second-year physicians at the bottom, and only one or two fifth-year Chief Residents at the top. This means that there are fewer positions to fill each year – say, ten to twelve intern spots, eight second-year positions, six third-year, and so on. Only those who make it through the full five-year program become Chiefs, and only Chiefs can qualify for board certification. If everyone who enrolls in the system intends to make it all the way to a rewarding and profitable surgical career, the program can become cutthroat in a hurry.

To me, this sort of competition seemed completely out of place in a patient care setting, especially in a teaching hospital. Intuitively, I felt that an academic medical center should be a place where seasoned practitioners reached out to mentor young charges, in a quiet environment where cooperation and mutual support ruled the day.

It didn't take long to find out that in surgery, such utopian views were held by a very tiny, very quiet minority.

As a practical matter, those of us at the entry level did work closely together, almost as a matter of survival. We shared tips on memorizing medical minutia and managing insane schedules, and navigating the personal idiosyncrasies of nurses, secretaries, senior residents and surgeons, building bonds of mutual reliance and in some cases deep friendships that have lasted for decades. Over time, however, the pressure of performing on rounds and exams, accumulating required experience points in the OR, the constant challenge of moving from one clinical discipline to the next, the endless workload, and the looming, ever-present specter of elimination through the pyramid process began to fray these interpersonal connections, often replacing them with feelings of suspicion and mistrust.

Fortunately, there was some wiggle room built into the system, so that the process was not always as merciless as it might otherwise have been. Some surgical interns were only expected to complete their first year of general surgery before moving on to more specialized training. Graduate doctors preparing for residencies in Ear, Nose & Throat or Orthopedics, for example, were required to finish a general surgical internship before beginning their specialty training. Some residents changed their minds, and withdrew voluntarily to pursue Internal Medicine, Anesthesia or Family Practice. Some bolted to outlying Emergency rooms, Doc-in-the-Boxes, or rural nursing home practices to lay low and make money while they sorted out their career plans. A few, like me, quit altogether, without having to be cut from the system. This is the Pyramid at work.

The system was cruelest to those who truly desired to become surgeons, in a program full of competitive cohorts. Many invested years of their lives performing the lowliest of tasks, only to be bumped off of the pyramid with no apology, and no safety net.

The process and goal of a surgical residency is similar in some respects to military boot camp: individual attitudes and thought processes are broken down through excessive labor, social deprivation, mental challenge and repetitive activity, then reformulated along a predetermined pattern to produce a reliable functional model. The process is legitimized and continually ingrained through the power of intimidation, the constant threat of dismissal, and the relentless momentum of tradition.

Ironically, even as it was working hard to discourage self-expression and originality, the program was actually encouraging me to be a creative problem-solver:

How am I going to do all this work?

How am I going to have any fun in the process?

How long can I put off answering this page?

How can I avoid another dressing-down from this Attending?

and

How in God's name am I going to keep from killing this patient?

Ultimately the training process also forced me to consider other career options. I certainly didn't enjoy my life as a resident. If I could find a way to make money and make a difference anywhere outside of the hospital, I was fast becoming open to the possibility.

Maybe I *could* be a writer, an editor, investigative reporter, researcher, detective, actor, salesman, social worker, teacher, a business administrator, civic leader, babysitter, or, if I had been paying attention, a comedian.

Or maybe I could roll all of them up together, I wondered, and be an artist.

Get Out

"...If you're looking for permission, this is it."

Out of the hospital, looking forward to a rare evening at home, I took a quick side trip to the grocery store to pick up something for dinner. I had not been on the job for very long, a few weeks, a month maybe, when I ran into a friendly acquaintance, the wife of one of the department chairmen here at the World Famous Medical Center. The family had been kind enough to put me up for a few days while I searched for an apartment earlier that summer. She was happy to see me now, excited to hear how my new life as a young doctor was going.

"Do you *love* it?" she gushed.

"I really hate it," I told her, reflexively. "Hate every minute of it, actually, aside from the few minutes a day I get to spend with patients." *Wow, that sounded harsh*, I thought, *even if it is true.* Let me try again: "I mean, I'm sure I'll get used to the routine, but right now it's pretty tough..."

Too late. Her warm smile had already collapsed. Given the unusual opportunity to speak freely with someone, instead of sharing a quiet confidence I blundered clumsily over some unmarked social boundary. Worse, I had let her down, and, from her cold expression, made her angry as well. She wasn't interested in hearing anything more.

"Get out," she told me, her voice chilled to a whisper.

Her turn to be harsh, I thought. Well, I had it coming, I guess.

"I mean it! Get out *now. Before it's too late*," she hissed, stepping uncomfortably close, her tone conspiratorial, urgent, as though we might be overheard.

Her sudden approach made me flinch. Surely she had to be kidding, exaggerating her reply for dramatic effect. That was it. She was making fun of me, parroting my own selfish overreaction to her polite question. How silly I must have sounded, so serious and pitiful.

Not so. Her demeanor hardened perceptibly as she began to share details from her own experience, recalling her marriage years earlier to a cheerful, optimistic young internist who, like me, had voiced deep concerns over his initial reactions to the burdensome process of resident training.

"He was so excited about being a doctor. *So* dedicated to his patients," she said, looking past me. "And what a *funny* guy he used to be!"

He used to be.

Over time she had watched the relentless pressure of her husband's career wear away his congenial personality, until it finally poisoned his relationships with everyone outside of the profession, including his family. He thought that he could wait it out, she told me, putting his personal feelings aside until he achieved a measure of authority within the academic community. Now he was at the top of the game, the leader of his chosen specialty, and he had become totally consumed by the job.

"He hasn't been the same in over twenty years," she told me, her eyes imploring me to pay attention. "*Believe* me, life is too short to throw it away on anything that doesn't make you happy."

She let go of my sleeve, and pulled away, slowly.

"Unless you are absolutely sure you love what you're doing, *get out while you can.*

Treating the Numbers

A nurse entered the operating room with a look of mild distress in her eyes, the only part of her face that was visible above her surgical mask. She stood quietly until the surgeon noticed her.

"What is it?" he said.

"It's your patient in 208, Doctor. His pressure is 82."

"Systolic?"

"Yes, Doctor."

The nurse was referring to Mr. Johnson, a patient we had operated on the previous week. We removed a small tumor from his lung, without difficulty, and until now without complications. He had long since been transferred out of Intensive Care to the main surgical floor, and that very morning we had removed last of the drainage tubes from his chest. He was scheduled to go home the next day.

Now his blood pressure was falling precipitously.

"Doctor Stewart, break scrub and go see what's going on. Nurse, grab that retractor."

Grateful for the break in a mind-numbing routine (in the O.R. the intern's job was to stand immobile for hours, holding the incision open while the surgeons worked), I stepped away from the table and out of the room, removing my sterile gown and gloves along the way. Running up the stairs to the second floor (surgical residents, like the military, take the steps two at a time), I hurried down the hallway toward Mr. J's room.

Normal resting blood pressure is 120 over 80. The higher number reflects the force of blood within the vessels when the heart
is beating. The lower number tells how much pressure remains
between the beats. Mr. Johnson's high number had just fallen
to two thirds its normal value. His low number was undetect-
able. That sudden loss of pressure meant that there was probably
a leak somewhere, and it was a big one. Mr. Johnson could be
bleeding to death internally.

There was no time to waste.

As I rushed along the hallway to his room, I thought through the
possibilities: The staples in his lung might have given way. Part
of his wound might have ruptured, leaking blood into his chest.
We may have ripped a small artery when we removed his chest
tubes earlier that morning. He might be suffering from a sudden, overwhelming infection, or an allergic reaction to one of his
medications. The stress of the surgery might have caused bleeding ulcers in Mr. J's stomach – or a heart attack. Whatever the
underlying cause, I expected to find my patient in bad shape: pale,
lightheaded, possibly unresponsive.

I tried to think ahead: Push IV fluids. Order blood transfusions.
Get an EKG – and a chest x-ray. Would he need emergency
surgery? Gastric endoscopy? Cardiac consult? Stool sample? Just
weeks out of medical school, all these tests and treatments were
bouncing around in my head like numbers in a lottery. And hiding there somewhere in the mix lurked the *real* problem, the one
I was sure I hadn't thought of, the one I might continue to miss
until after my patient had expired.

First things first: Examine the wound. Listen to the patient's
chest. Check his temperature. See if his blood pressure has stabi-
lized, or is still falling.

I rounded the corner to room 208, knocked and entered, then
stopped short, shocked at the scene that greeted me.

Past Medical History

Mr. Johnson was sitting up in bed, smiling and chatting with his wife. His skin was pink. His lips were rosy red. His eyes were clear.

He said he was feeling fine, and I believed him.

"No lightheadedness?"

"No."

"No new pain or distress?"

"None."

"No complaints at all?"

"None at all – except that the nurse keeps bothering me about taking my blood pressure."

Right on cue, the RN rolled in a portable blood-pressure cuff. "Doctor, I'm glad you're here. This patient's pressure has been hovering around 80," she said. "Something needs to be done - quickly."

I hesitated, confused, trying to reconcile her concern with Mr. Johnson's obvious state of health.

"Check it yourself!" she said, thrusting the apparatus toward me.

Just then an orderly leaned in. He gave the nurse a sideways glance, and said, "That cuff's readings have been all over the map. It needs to be fixed, or thrown out."

Utter relief washed over me. The long list of possible diagnoses, complications and treatments wafted out of my mind, replaced by an enveloping sense of calm - a rare experience for a surgical intern.

I bade Mr. Johnson goodbye and told him that we'd return in a few hours for evening rounds.

Back in the OR, I gave my report:

"The patient was fine."

"What was his blood pressure?" asked the surgeon.

"I didn't check it. The cuff was broken, and right then there wasn't another one available on the floor."

"What did his lungs sound like?"

"I didn't listen to them. He was sitting up and talking, with no shortness of breath, no anxiety, no distress."

"How was his wound?"

"I didn't see it. The nurse had just applied a fresh dressing; she said that it looked fine."

"What was his temperature?"
"I glanced at his chart. His temp was normal a half-hour ago, and it's been stable for days."

The surgeon looked up at me sharply, eyes blazing over the top of his mask. His reaction shook the room.

"You *didn't* examine your patient? You *didn't* check his blood pressure? You *didn't even bother to take his temperature?!*"

He doctor wasted no time telling me how this level of neglect and incompetence could mean the end of my patient, and portended a similar prognosis for my medical career. I was ordered to return to the floor immediately, conduct the indicated tests, and report back in short order.

Of course I complied – only this time, I took the stairs one at a time.

A thorough exam revealed that the patient's blood pressure was normal. His wound looked fine. His lungs were clear. His temperature was 98.6...

My initial assessment was confirmed to the satisfaction of the floor nurse and the attending surgeon. But the importance of my being able to make that assessment, based on my own powers of observation and clinical judgment, had somehow gotten lost in the numbers.

The surgeon was right about one thing. In the new era of defensive medicine, with its increasing demand for objective data, the kind of medicine I had looked forward to practicing was quickly slipping into history.

In every sense, my days as a doctor were numbered.

Exit Signs

I really didn't mind the idea of being a surgeon. Surely at some point I even wanted to be one.

I had the hands of a surgeon. I had a surgeon's ego. I even thought like a surgeon, approaching problems with a solution in mind, and a clear, well-defined path toward a desired outcome. I had the practical desire to separate my patients physically from their diseases, in the shortest possible time, and get them back to their normal lives with minimal need for ongoing medical intervention.

The real problem for me was that, after medical school, there just wasn't time to do anything else *but* surgery. Apparently there never would be, either, ever again.

I missed my garden, and fishing, and hours in the kitchen cooking big, complicated meals for a houseful of friends. I missed reading non-medical books, and television, and all the things that require quiet time, uninterrupted by pagers and phone calls and endless hours on the wards. I missed poetry. More than anything, I missed my inalienable right to stay up late doing nothing in particular, and waste entire weekends if I felt like it (and believe me, there were times when I felt like doing nothing else).

I missed drawing, too.

Not that I had ever spent much time doing it. Nor that I ever really considered myself particularly adept. Back in college I thoroughly enjoyed my basic studio art class, squandering many an afternoon in a harmless diversion that led unexpectedly to additional classes in drawing and design. All good fun at the time, but hardly the stuff to contribute to an aspiring medical career. Definitely no substitute for a real job.

No, art was definitely a sideline. Along with acting and gardening and woodcraft, drawing had to be packed neatly away among the other nonessential aspects of carefree living until medical school, residency and fellowship could be dealt with, a practice established, nurtured, expanded and defended from the ravages of inevitable lawsuits and anonymous third party payors. Maybe in my later years there would be time to draw, after the important stuff was taken care of. When I retired, perhaps, my art would be there waiting for me, like a patient old friend.

So why, my internship barely begun, did I find myself standing in the middle of a Big Box store, writing a check for a 3x4 foot drawing table and a raft of art supplies that I would never get to use?

When you buy a shiny new hammer and a box of nails, it means that you're serious about building something. Even if you have no idea what it is going to be.

Happy?

The nurse stared at me over the tops of her dark-rimmed glasses, idly tapping a pencil against her chin.

"When was the last time you were happy, Dr. Stewart?" she asked.

She sat behind the counter at the central nurses' station in the Med/Surg wing, the step-down unit for patients who had been released from intensive care, and hopefully would be on their way home soon. Her question stopped me, mid-thought, distracting me from whatever problem I was struggling with between pager beeps. I looked up from my patient's chart to see what on earth she was talking about. She just stared back at me, waiting for me to answer.

Happy?

It was an unfair question, on its face. Residents were not supposed to be happy. Interns weren't allowed. The fact that she chose to pierce the veil of professional propriety and ask the question – indeed, the fact that she cared enough to inquire as to an intern's feelings at all was enough to pull me up short, and force me to consider coming up with an answer. Whether her query came from a place of compassion for me as a fellow human being, or the likelihood that she was simply fed up with my consistently crappy attitude I didn't know, though I suspect it was the latter.

Happy?

The answer popped into my head instantly, without effort: Five years. Five years exactly. Long before this gig. Before med school, even.

The awareness was accompanied by a clear, cinematic image, floating somewhere just behind my forehead, illuminated indirectly by the memory of north-facing, floor-to-ceiling windows.

Five years.

Half a decade of putting on a good face, trying to make yourself believe that your life was on track, that you'd gotten your wish. That you were doing what you wanted to be doing. And if you weren't feeling good about it all the time, at least you were working toward the day that you would be. Some day. Some day soon, maybe, but more than likely some time after your training was over, when you could settle down and establish a practice, raise a family, and finally get on with the business of living your life...

Best not to think about it now. There's too much work to do.

The answer, though, was five years.

"Five years," I told her. "It was five years ago." The picture persisted on the screen at the front of my mind.

She gasped, just a little. I don't believe she expected so prompt a response to her mostly rhetorical question. Certainly not one so direct, or so specific.

"I was back in college," I said, reminiscing. "Sitting in the art studio, working on a drawing. No interruptions. Not a care in the world. That's the last time I was happy."

The memory shines as bright and clear today as it did then. Studio 4, Basic Drawing Class, Final Exam Project: "Execute a design, a single illustration of a recognizable form, composed of multiple smaller images, in the style of Arcimboldo."

That project scared the living hell out of me.

Art class was supposed to be easy, a cakewalk for a pre-med. Draw a picture, get a grade. The closer you were able to accurately represent the model in front of you, the better that grade would be. Make it pretty. Move on.

But this assignment, this *exam*, had thrown things completely off track.

Finding something to draw was not the issue. All you had to do was leaf through a magazine and pick a decent photo – or set up a tray of plastic fruit, wooden blocks, crumpled butcher paper. No problem at all. After that, you went through the steps of visually deconstructing the various design elements of your model, assessing spatial and tonal relationships, and reproducing those associations on paper. Beer then, done that, dozens of times.

This project was different. Here we would be required to generate an image, deconstruct the elements within that design, and then build them back using a *dozen other drawings* – each with its own qualities, each interacting visually with every other shape around it. The planning alone was tantamount to researching a term paper, an exercise in Left-Brain calisthenics that was rarely encountered in the Department of Art. Finding a way to make this kind of a drawing *work*, to balance visually, to 'read' in the end as a single entity, was enough to make my Right Brain run and hide – or spit on its palms, clap them together, and wade headlong into the contest.

The prospect of using both sides of my brain simultaneously represented a new challenge all by itself. I was used to *thinking*. Absorbing, processing, and regurgitating facts was the business of a science major. I was also used to *creating*, mentally shaping ideas and forms and placing them meaningfully on the page. That was art.

Performing both acts at once wasn't just unusual, it was utterly terrifying – and wonderfully exhilarating...

"Yeah, that would be it. The last time I was really happy."

"I didn't know you were an artist," she said.

"I'm not," I replied. "I'm an intern."

Final Exam

One Saturday afternoon in early fall, all the interns were called into a small auditorium, the same room where we attended weekly staff presentations, Grand Rounds, M&M* conferences, etc. We were instructed to remain silent, while secretaries in crisp skirts and dark blazers passed out sharpened number two pencils and sealed test packets blazoned with the World Famous Medical Center logo.

"This is your first practice board exam," we were told. "You have one hour to complete the test."

Breaking the seal on my thick white folder, I discovered that this was indeed a collection of bona fide, official exam sheets, all sanctioned by the American College of Surgeons, one of several such fauxams the full-timers could expect to face each year through the course of their training. The questions had been culled from previous board exams, that massive test we would one day be required to pass in order to become *Board Certified* – qualified to practice the ancient science and art of surgery in America's hospitals. The questions in this particular packet all had to do with Vascular Surgery, that branch of the profession that dealt with clogged arteries, varicose veins, bypass grafts and the like.

This is not going to be pretty, I thought to myself. In medical school we received very little training on the subject, save for basic vascular anatomy in a course I completed with barely adequate grades a full four years earlier. As a student I was allowed to watch a bloody varicose vein stripping and a couple of arterial graft procedures, one tube sewn onto another, but that was the extent of my clinical experience on the subject.

---

*Morbidity and Mortality Conference: a monthly meeting where staff physicians and senior residents were called on the carpet to explain suboptimal clinical outcomes for patients under their care.

Already confident, then, of the outcome of this exam, I allowed my anxiety to take a rest for a while, and settled in for an hour of luxuriant failure.

My ignorance of the subject matter had been highlighted and underscored, daily, in every aspect of my current position. Six or seven weeks into the intern program, after caroming through a series of truncated general surgery services (it was summertime, and many of the staff surgeons had upset the usual training schedule with out-of-town conferences and personal vacations), I had finally been assigned to my first full rotation on a busy Thoracic and Vascular surgery practice.

Busy was the operative word. Chest tumors, foreign bodies, vessel malformations, aortic aneurysms, trauma... With the exception of open-heart surgery, if it traversed the chest and needed removal or renovation, we were the team to do it.

It is worth noting that patients who show up with lung and large vessel problems usually inhabit bodies with lots of miles on them. More often than not, these are folks who also suffer from one or more of the other diseases associated with advancing age: diabetes, high blood pressure, kidney failure, atherosclerosis, COPD, arthritis. Most of our patients were already queuing up opposite Death's door, with or without the ailment that brought them to ours. Their complicated health histories were the main reason we were seeing them in the first place. If these operations had been easy, their local surgeons would have done them already, on their way to the golf course. (Or so we were led to believe, as a matter of pride. The easy cases never made it to the WFMC. That was why we were the *best*.) By the time we finished cracking open elderly chests and digging around for an hour or two, whether or not our patients would even wake up the next day became a legitimate question.

My qualifications for managing these people after surgery? A still-damp diploma, and a pulse. "Here's your pager, Don. Good luck."

Good luck, indeed.

Overnight, I became responsible for the lives of thirty critically ill patients, ten or more of them in Intensive Care, most of these kept alive solely through the efforts of incredibly talented ICU nurses whose job, frighteningly enough, was to follow *my* orders. Two months out of medical school, I hardly knew a pressor from a dilator. This was a real problem, since my ICU patients had a stream of each drug flowing into them simultaneously, tightening and relaxing their blood vessels in a tug-of-war to maintain a stable, viable pressure. Angelic nursing staff spent the night watching the numbers, along with ventilator settings, blood gases, IV fluids, antibiotics, diuretics, pain meds, cold compresses, warm blankets and whatever else the patients needed to give their traumatized bodies the greatest probability of surviving until morning. If they made it that far, chances were that they would make it home in a wheelchair, rather than a hearse.

Every other day we would operate, sometimes on as many as eight patients in a row. Every night I would do my best to keep those people breathing and circulating and peeing, mindless of my own blood pressure and respiratory rates. I didn't have time to pee.

On "non-operative" days, I would transfer the healthiest of the recovering ICU patients down to the surgical wing of the hospital, where they could heal in relative peace. Hopefully on those days I would also be able to discharge an equal number of my other postoperative patients home, before preparing the paperwork for a new crop of pre-ops who were already on their way over from the clinic. Mornings and evenings every day, I had to look in on all of my patients, first by myself, then with the senior resident, and finally with the staff surgeon. All day and well into the night, my pager would alert me for ICU orders, laboratory and radiology reports, questions and concerns of nurses, family, pharmacy, calls from the clinic, calls from consultants, calls from outside physicians, and update requests from senior house staff.

During high-traffic periods, it would buzz endlessly for an hour or longer, assuring me of enough follow-up work to keep me awake and occupied for most of the night, every night.

I did my best to keep up, and most days everything got done - but there was simply too much work for one underqualified scut-monkey to handle. Those nights when I slept at all, I slept fitfully, hoping against the odds that I hadn't managed to kill anyone that day.

With nearly two whole weeks of vascular experience under my belt, I sat down to take my practice test:

No, I did not remember the origin of the anterior meningeal artery, or the common anatomic variations of the splanchnic vessels. I did not know the comparative long-term complications of the several treatments of varicose veins, or the difference between a mamillary and a papillary artery, or the specific indications for surgical intervention in chronic limb ischemia. Then again, I didn't feel I needed to. Not yet anyway. I was just beginning a five-year adventure in surgery. These fun facts and more would be brought to my attention over the course of my training, wouldn't they? I settled down and answered the questions, filling in the little circles as best I could. Surprisingly, there were no questions asking about routine blood work, urine output, chest tubes, dressing changes, admission histories, progress notes, prescriptions, consoling worried families, or dictating discharge summaries – the things that filled my days to capacity, things I had actually become quite good at doing.

Clearly, the purpose of this exam was not to identify my strong points, but to make me aware of the deficits in my fund of surgical knowledge, as an incentive to study and learn more in the days to come. After all, how can you learn anything if you don't know you don't know it? Now I knew. And one of these days, when I had a little sleep and enough time to manage my basic bodily functions, I would get back into the swing of academic pursuits. One day soon. Why, I might even grab a book right now and... Nope, there went the pager again.

Off the Pharm

"You can't just *leave*," I said.

"Why not? It's my career. It's my life."

He said these things so matter-of-factly, they almost sounded true.

Jim was a third year medical student, visiting from somewhere in Ohio, or Illinois. Maybe it was Indiana. At 29, this was not his first pass through the education mill. Jim had a Pharm.D. degree, and had already seen his research published in major medical journals. He was spending a couple of weeks visiting our program to investigate the possibility of one day becoming a surgeon himself. Three days into the experience, he had made up his mind.

"Why do you let them treat you this way?" he asked me that morning. We were sitting across from one another, perched on opposite beds in the call room, having just completed a sleepless night of post-operative activity, followed by morning rounds, breakfast, and post-prandial scut work. The afternoon promised a mandatory lecture on the Risk/Benefit Ratio of the Such-and-Forth Maneuver, before we started doing intake exams for tomorrow's procedures.

"This is just the way it's done, I suppose," I told him. "You have to prove you're good enough to join the ranks. That you're up to the challenge of being a surgeon."

"So if you take enough crap, you automatically qualify to be one of these guys? How fucked up is that?"

"The argument we hear all the time around here is *'Tradition'*. They had to go through it, and that means we do, too."

"Maybe *you* do. Like I said, that's fucked up."

"The other residents will tell you the program builds character. Makes you a man," I said, with what I hoped was a conspiratorial grin. It was a weak conspiracy. *Resignation* might have been a better word for it.

Jim wasn't smiling. "I don't have to prove my manhood to any of these assholes," he said. "I already have 'Doctor' in front of my name. So do you, for that matter. We shouldn't have to put up with this kind of abuse from anyone, least of all from people who are supposed to be teaching us how to care about our patients." He paused for a moment, contemplating the small patch of floor between his shoes. "*Prove* we're good enough to be surgeons. Huh," he said, with a sad grin of his own. "When I could be at home, actually learning something right now."

With that he levered himself up and left the room, heading down the hall toward the coffee machine. I waited a while for him to come back, but after a moment or two my pager went off, and I reached around to the desk to grab the phone. A minute later I was lost in the momentum of the job.

The next morning I was called out of surgery, and ordered downtown to the Registrar's office. The Assistant Associate in charge of the Visiting Scholars program was waiting to see me. She wanted to know what was wrong with my medical student.

"What do you mean?"

"Wasn't he feeling well? Perhaps there was a family emergency?"

"Yes. No... Not that I know of. Why?"

"Well, he came in here yesterday afternoon and turned in his ID badge. He said that he was leaving the program early. He was going home."

"Yes, ma'am."

"But he had, let's see… more than a week to go with his visit."

"Yes, that's right."

"Was there a reason he left early?"

"I guess he'd just had enough."

"What do you mean?" She was genuinely puzzled.

"You're kidding, right?" I said simply, momentarily dropping all pretense of professional decorum. Maybe she really needed an answer, needed to explain this behavioral anomaly to someone higher up in her chain of command, but if this was a problem, it wasn't mine. Jim stopped being my responsibility the minute he walked out of the call room. He was gone. He was home free. I would be stuck in this place for years.

This lady was not a doctor, or a patient, a nurse or even a ward clerk. At the moment, she was a midlevel administrative functionary whose curiosity was keeping me from getting a whole lot of work done.

"The way they treat surgical residents here, are you really surprised that he's gone? This is a pretty awful existence."

Her puzzlement turned to shock. "We have one of the finest surgical programs in the world!" she sputtered.

"I guess that tells you how dismal the rest of them are, then," I said, coloring the phrase with just a hint of her own Midwestern dialect.

She stood across the counter, gaping, looking like she'd just been slapped, which I guess she had.

Wow, I thought to myself. *This is one conversation that's bound to show up somewhere in my file.* "Will there be anything else?" I asked.

"No," she said, recovering her composure, her expression now shifting from surprise to righteous anger. "Thank you."

I was already on my way out the door, back to the shuttle van, to the hospital, to a backlog of charts and pages and lab orders and afternoon rounds – things that Jim wouldn't have to worry about anymore.

Lucky bastard.

I was sure there would be a note added to his medical school file as well; a brief, effusive letter on official WFMC stationery relating how happy they were that he chose to visit our facility and train with our staff, how well he performed and how pleased they would be if he ranked our surgical program #1 in the residency matching process.

I Quit

My surgical staff advisor called me at home on a Sunday evening
– the one night when, every other week, the on-call schedule allowed me to sleep in my own bed. The occasion for his call was to
review my performance on a recent practice exam, to tell me that I
had made a C on a test covering material I basically knew nothing
about.

I was ecstatic. He was not.

We expect far more from our residents, he went on to say, than
merely *average performance*. He had been watching me closely on
rounds, he continued, and in the OR, and during lectures and conferences. He had a sense that I wasn't quite fitting in.

This was bad news – the worst review a surgical resident could
expect to hear from a superior, short of outright malpractice. It
meant that unless I recognized and corrected whatever was keeping me from blending seamlessly with the training program, I could
expect to be let go at the end of the year. Possibly sooner.

At the time I was the lone junior resident on a busy vascular surgery service, which meant that I was responsible for managing
thirty patients around the clock, up to a third of them in Critical
Care. I was seven, maybe eight weeks out of medical school, with
only a rudimentary understanding of medications and procedures
required to keep any of these people alive. Hard as I tried, it was
impossible to acquire knowledge and experience fast enough to do
my job effectively, and some of the daily burden was being shifted
up the line to the senior residents. This was inexcusable.

I was apparently expected to know much more than I actually did:
More details of anatomy. More physiology. More pharmacology.

More general medicine. Certainly more surgery. The majority of these things I was supposed to have learned long before I arrived. The rest I was to have absorbed or figured out on my own, in daily conferences, on rounds, in the OR, or studying in the call room between beeper pages, before falling asleep at the end of another eighteen-to-twenty-two-hour workday.

As medical students and residents, it was our responsibility to build and maintain an adequate *Fund of Knowledge,* equivalent to that of our professional peer group – a group that included every other surgeon, everywhere in the world. If they knew it, we were supposed to know it. In other words, we were responsible for *everything.*

Adding to the difficulty was my attitude toward medical practice in general, which had not yet begun to recover from my overall disillusionment with medical school.

Perhaps my daily panic to keep up was what the advisor was referring to. His phone call was intended to whip me into shape, to motivate me to push harder, study more, learn to work more efficiently in order to maintain my position in the program.

"You know, you may not be cut out to be a surgeon," he said finally, completely missing the irony in his choice of words. "Take some time to think about it, and get back to me when you have decided what you plan to do."

We both understood that I was never supposed to get back to him. I was supposed to pick myself up by my bootstraps, put my shoulder to the wheel, press my nose to the grindstone, lift my share of the load, keep my mouth shut, and soldier on. He would be able to see my newfound determination by my improved behavior on the wards.

I called him back an hour later.

That in itself was a flagrant breach of academic etiquette, adding one more item to my list of professional shortcomings. Only senior residents were allowed to contact staff surgeons at home, and then only in times of emergency.

"I've been thinking about what you told me, sir, and I'm afraid I have to agree with you," I began.

"Well, that's more like — "

"Apparently I am *not* cut out to be a surgeon."

I explained that according to his own assessment, I was unable to meet the levels of responsibility and performance that my current assignment required, and that with such a heavy caseload, my patients were not getting the standard of care they deserved. Best for everyone that I step aside now, and allow someone more qualified to do the job.

There. I'd said it. Out loud. All of his suspicions and accusations were confirmed. We were now on the same page, *finally*. His troubles, with me at least, were over.

Which is why his response, when it came, was so unexpected.

Rather than join me in a sigh of mutual relief, he suddenly became even more agitated. "That was not what I meant *at all*," he exclaimed. "I was just trying to get you to work harder! You're a *doctor*, for God's sake. You can't just walk away from that!"

Where the hell was *this* coming from? Of course I could walk away. I believe I just had. Tomorrow I would report to the administrative office and turn in my resignation. My patients would no longer be at risk, and I would be free to find something I else I could do with my life that would make me and him a lot happier. It was a win-win.

He urged me again to reconsider. We would talk more about it in the morning.

Talk about what? I was baffled, but he insisted. Fine. I'd see him tomorrow morning.

I slept better that night than I had in months.

At six a.m. I was summoned to an impromptu meeting downtown, on the surgical floor of the clinic building. The assistant director of the department, the head of Vascular Surgery, and my faculty advisor were all waiting to speak with me – an imposing panel of internationally recognized physicians who ordinarily would not waste a minute of their time on the troubles of an intern.

I suspected that they were going to fire me, rather than allow me to resign on my own. But what would be the benefit in that? Any secretary could hand me a letter of dismissal, take away my clinic ID card, and with it, my hospital privileges. Surely these men had more important things to do with their morning than discharge an entry-level employee. Yet here they were, the three of them, sitting across the table from me in a small meeting room, carefully reviewing my decision to leave.

Surprisingly this did not turn into a grilling, like on rounds, or even a personal dressing-down. On the contrary, their approach was eerily supportive. "Why do you want to leave medicine?" they asked. "What sorts of things have been bothering you? How can we help get things back on track?"

I was stunned. The most I expected to hear from these guys was a repeat of all the reasons why I did not belong in the hospital, with maybe a forced, cordial farewell and a tepid smile: '*Good luck and no hard feelings - really.*' What I got instead was fifteen minutes of genuine concern, though even then I was under no illusion that the concern was actually for *me*.

While this meeting did little to quell my misgivings toward the job or my ability to perform it, or my career in general, for that matter, it did give me some critical insights into the priorities of the resident training program. The base of the resident pyramid, I discovered, was fundamental to the functioning of the entire system. Without eight warm bodies on the receiving end of eight intern pagers, somebody else would have to do the daily paperwork, chase down lab numbers and keep up with the patients. I was a grunt, and grunts had their place – mainly keeping those higher up on the pyramid from sliding one notch back down toward the bottom. There is some comfort in that, and an odd sense of job security in playing an essential supportive role, however ignored or maligned one might feel in the trenches of daily duty. It was a creepy kind of comfort, but it was better than nothing, I guessed.

Nobody told me this. Certainly none of the three eminent physicians evaluating me that morning told me that my position was important, or necessary, or that my presence in their hospital was even particularly desirable. Their comments were couched in terms of my own benefit: I had come a long way down a difficult path. I had been given a cherished opportunity, one not to be discarded lightly. I had a solemn responsibility to my *patients*.

All true. All reasons for me to choose to stick it out for the rest of the year. But none of these observations addressed the central argument that I was somehow academically inferior – their words, not mine – for if I were truly incapable of being a good surgeon, why were they so eager to keep me on board? That question was never addressed.

In the end, they reminded me of one important consideration. A medical student must complete at least one year of postgraduate training before any of the fifty United States will grant him or her a license to practice. If I quit before then, I would lose my chance to be credentialed. The future is uncertain, the committee told me, and it would be a shame to have come so far down the road toward being a doctor, to dedicate that much time and energy, and never have the choice to practice – should I someday decide I wanted to do so. Better to stay on, they reasoned, and at least complete my internship. If you make it through this, they said, you can make it through anything. And who knows? Once you get the toughest year behind you, you'll probably feel like the rest is not so hard.

So I stayed, for a time with the benefit of increased supervision as my skills improved, and the difficult rotation through vascular surgery came to a welcome end. After that I was sent to perform six weeks' penance in the colon and rectal clinic, working under a cloud of suspicion and shame, the mark of a lame duck intern – a surgical Shit Bird.

That was fine, for now I had a goal: Earn my license. All I had to do was survive the rest of the year, struggling to work in concert with the prime Hippocratic directive: *First Do No Harm* – either to my patients, or, now, to myself.

What would happen after that? I didn't know. By then I could see no place in the broad spectrum of medical practice where I cared to spend the remaining years of my productive life, and that was fine, too. I would sit for my medical board exams with a sense of placid resignation, understanding that for me, the attainment of licensure would be an end in itself.

Shit Bird

When a joke is really good, it doesn't matter if you find yourself at the butt end.

Shortly after my first, aborted attempt to leave hospital, residency and medical career behind, the front office sent me an updated course schedule. The surgical rotations I had been assigned at the beginning of the year had all been changed: Some were postponed until later in the year. Others had been eliminated altogether, with additional services added in their places.

Now, instead of moving on to a six-week term in Neurosurgery, I was ordered to report to the Colon & Rectal Clinic, where I had been reassigned to the sigmoidoscopy room.

This special outpost dealt with the fundamentals of surgical medicine: Hemorrhoids. Fissures. Fistulas and abscesses. Colon and rectal cancers. The running joke at the time (among many) was that we treated our patients from the bottom up.

Since many of these disorders would be discovered during a routine physical exam, the serious cases were sent directly to the operating room. Few patients with acute rectal complaints were considered appropriate candidates for sigmoidoscopy. Instead, this endoscopic procedure was generally reserved for those with chronic complaints, e.g. a prior history of colon cancer, or who otherwise needed to be screened for tumors, ulcers and other diseases commonly found in the lower portion of the digestive tract.

My job was to gently place a long, stainless steel tube (shiny as a chrome hood ornament, nicknamed the Silver Bullet) ten inches deep into a patient's rectum, turn on the light, and take a quick look around.

Except for the occasional biopsy, there wasn't much else to the procedure. Get a good look, dictate a report, and get out while the nurse prepped the room for the next patient. On a good day we could manage a dozen cases or more.

The Pooper Clinic was intended to be a punitive assignment, a clear message from the residency administrators that I had become a pain in the ass. One doesn't thumb one's nose at the gift of medical training. Rather, one must do all one can to get that nose good and brown. This was to be a lesson in subservience.

Looking at butt holes all day should have been all that was needed to adjust my attitude, turn me around, and shame me back onto the path of surgical righteousness. Like so much of my medical experience, though, it just didn't work out that way.

Instead, the Silver Bullet service turned into a resident's dream: Nine to five. A full hour for lunch. No weekend duty. *No call.* For a month and a half, I felt like a human being again. Hell, I felt like I was on *vacation.* For the first time in years, I had time at the end of the day to do whatever I wanted.

It didn't matter that my superiors had banished me from the OR. I was racking up more reportable operations* in a single day than I was allowed to perform on any of my other six-week rotations. And with so much daily repetition, I was actually getting good at the procedure. By the end of my tenure in the Colon Clinic, I had completed more than 300 rectal exams, and, ironically, done away with much of my crappy attitude.

I also had time to start working on my first serious drawing since college. The clinic office windows looked out upon the most or-

*An important part of surgical training was the accumulation of required experience points, which were based on the number and type of procedures performed over the course of one's residency. Board certification required every resident to participate in a minimum number of cases in each of the various specialties.

nate examples of architecture in the entire medical center, a complex of sculptural images so engaging that it inspired a lifelong series of drawings. I often spent my lunch hour staring out the window and sketching, a practice that before long set me onto an entirely new career path.

Another unexpected benefit to working in the Butt Clinic came from a most unlikely source – the Queen of the CRC, Nurse Peregrine herself.

Nurse P ruled the Colon and Rectal Clinic with steel talons, and decades of experience withering residents and full-fledged surgeons alike with her icy, menacing glare. No one dared run afoul of her, and few residents made it through a full rotation without feeling the sting of her wrath.

The afternoon she craned her head unexpectedly into the treatment room, my sphincter pressure instantly rose higher than my patient's.

"I would like to see you when you have a moment, Doctor," she said ominously.

Tall, taut and bird-boned, a ravenous raptor poised to descend, dissect, and devour, Nurse P. motioned for me to follow her to her office. Once inside, she turned to me with a serious look on her face, variations of which were the only expressions I knew her to have.

"My husband is a patient here," she said, matter-of-factly. "Since his colon cancer five years ago, he has had a sigmoid exam every six months, usually performed by a resident."

Her expression hardened, whether in thought or anger I couldn't tell. I waited in terror for the axe to fall.

Whatever I had done, it was bad, and I had done it to her *spouse.*

My ass was in a sling now, tucked tight and ready for launch.

Peregrine's husband was apparently the "secret shopper" of the colon clinic, his job to report on the inadequacies of interns on Pooper duty. In spite of the relaxed schedule, we still walked on eggshells in this place, terrified that we might inadvertently impale our patients with a blunt metal instrument the size of a dinner candle, or worse – commit some procedural error that would turn Nurse Peregrine's unwelcome attention in our direction.

Now I discover that *Mr.* Peregrine was scouting us out, evaluating our technique, then serving us up to his Missus for sacrifice.

"You performed the exam on him last Tuesday, Dr. Stewart."

Of course I did. I was the only one on permanent shit duty that month. Now that assignment was about to permanently perfume what was left of my tattered residency. Slowly the lines in her face relaxed, and the corners of her mouth turned upward in a warm and pleasant smile. Holy *shit!* Now I was *really* scared.

"He just wanted me to tell you that he didn't feel a thing," she said. "No pain, no discomfort whatsoever. This was the only time that has happened in all the years he has had to endure the procedure."

She paused for a moment for this to sink in, allowing me to regain my composure.

"I just wanted to thank you," she continued. "You apparently are very good at this job."

It truly was nice of her to say so, I thought, and not just because I had been anticipating a thorough ass-kicking. Interns so seldom receive positive feedback from any of their superiors, and kudos from Nurse P. were rare indeed.

I walked home that day an inch off the ground, and kept her encouraging comments with me for the rest of the year. It wasn't enough to make me want to stay, but whenever the going got really tough, a tiny part of me could rest confidently in the understanding there was at least one thing in all of my surgical experience that I could do, and do well. Nurse Peregrine said so.

That part of my journey is still worth celebrating, and I do, even today. Whenever someone raises a glass to toast any occasion, Nurse P. invariably crosses my mind, and I can't help but smile, just a little bit.

("Bottoms up!")

Find the X-Ray

There are two inviolable rules in a surgical internship:

> Rule #1: You know nothing.

> Rule #2: You are responsible for everything.

My pager goes off again, like it has a dozen times, at least, in the last half hour.

It's the end of the day. A non-operative day. A Clinic Day, which means that while the senior members of the team are across town seeing new patients and follow-ups, I am here at the hospital, trying to make sure the people we operated on yesterday are still alive, and getting ready to admit another wave of new cases.

I walk ten paces to the telephone, one of five or six on the cluttered table next to the nurse's station, and punch the number displayed on the pager's tiny LCD screen. I pull out a pen and blank sheet of chart paper, and prepare to take notes.

"Are you ready?" asks the senior resident, who reads from his own handwritten notes, collected on 3x5 cards during the course of the day. "Jones, Cecil. 58 year-old white male with left upper lobar mass. Thoracotomy. Next. Samuelsen, Alice. 62 year-old white female with hilar adenopathy. Biopsy. Next..."

As an intern, my place is here in the hospital. Staff physicians and higher-ranking residents spend alternate days seeing patients over at the Clinic and down in the OR. I spend my time in the hallways, wards and ICUs, admitting referrals one day, holding retractors the next, and answering the pager around the clock.

On admission days I examine patients who have already been fully examined, fill out hospital charts that mirror clinic charts, order lab work that has already been scheduled, write prescriptions that have been written for me to write again, and round up stray test results – all clearly outlined in orders previously documented, and sent over from the clinic for disposition. I am a radio dish, a catcher's mitt, a dustpan. I sweep in the cumulus of the day, then funnel, sort, and arrange it all in an orderly fashion before surgery the following morning. God help me if something that has already been done elsewhere and in triplicate isn't done again, in proper order, by me.

I have already put in a twelve-hour day. By the time these new patients start arriving, I have twelve hours left to get them admitted, examined, charted and prepped – and try to get some sleep before my work day starts again at five a.m.

Let's be clear about this: I have never seen anything or anyone that is being transferred to me today from the clinic. Until it arrives at the hospital, to the nurse's station on my floor, I have no way of knowing if it even exists. I have never met these patients. I have not yet read their charts. I do not know what labs, bloodwork, or procedural tests have been ordered, or whether these tests have been completed. I have not seen the results.

This is the condition imposed by Rule #1.

Nevertheless, according to Rule #2, I am personally responsible for the acquisition, processing, safe transport, and ultimate disposition of all materials ordered by others on behalf of their, soon to be our, patients. It is my job to see that all pertinent data and test results are ready and available when each of these patients is wheeled into surgery the following day.

"… and make sure we have the x-ray on Jones," says the Senior, signing off on his report from the clinic.

It's now after five o'clock. The clinic is closed. The shuttle from the clinic building to the hospital has made its last run of the day. My patients begin to show up for admission: Ratliff, Nelson, Samuelsen, Jones... They arrive with their paperwork and their orders. The lab pages me relentlessly with their latest test results, in no particular order: blood counts, electrolytes, glucose levels, urinalyses. Additional deliveries bring printouts of EKGs, pulmonary function tests, CT scans, and radiographs to the floor, to my attention.

An hour of busy work clicks by, and it's time to see Mr. Jones. 58 yowm*. Smoker. Upper left pulmonary mass discovered on a routine chest x-ray, which somehow did not make the trip over from the Clinic. I recall Senior's emphatic instruction:

"... make sure we have the x-ray on Jones."

I look again. No film. I sort through the envelopes that came over with my other patients. Nothing. I ask the unit clerk if she's seen a stray x-ray. No luck.

There is a technical term we residents have for this kind of development. It's called *Not Good*.

I call the Senior, who is now in ICU checking on the progress of yesterday's cases. "Mr. Jones came over without his chest x-ray. Any idea where he left it?"

"It was on the box in the exam room. That's the last I saw of it."

"What do I do now?"

"Find it." He hangs up.

---

*58 yowm: 58 year-old white male.

I call the radiology department at the clinic. It's closed. I leave a message on the recorder.

I call the radiology desk at the hospital. They resent the fact that I am questioning their ability to deliver the film. "If it came over, it went up to the floor."

"If it didn't come over, where would it be?"

"How should I know? Call the clinic office."

"They're closed."

"Call 'em in the morning. They open at seven."

"We have to be in surgery at seven."

"Sounds like you've got a problem." That part I know.

I finish tucking in Mr. Jones, then head for the door. "Where are you going?" the nurse calls after me. She knows how much work I had left to do.

"To the clinic."

I make my way to the parking lot, jealous of the time I am losing, and hoping my absence from the hospital won't be noticed. The last thing I need is to get called in on a critical patient while I'm AWOL, looking for a lousy chest film. I drive over to the clinic, where my Medical Center ID card gets me in the door. The security guard escorts me up to the surgical floor, follows me from room to room. All the light boxes are empty. There are no x-rays loose at the nurse's station, no manila envelopes marked 'Jones" lying on desktops or counters, or anywhere else in the facility that I can find. I am not allowed in to the radiology office.

"Call 'em in the morning," suggests the guard.

Back at the hospital, I wolf down a sandwich for dinner, and head back up to the floor to tackle the rest of the paperwork, and begin answering a backlog of pages.

"Where have you been hiding?" Senior wants to know.

"Looking for Mr. Jones' CXR."

"You find it?"

"Nope."

"Find it."

I make one more trip downstairs to the radiology desk. They never saw Mr. Jones' film. They have no record of it being sent over from the clinic. They don't want me to bother them about it any more, *is that clear.*

That could not be clearer. The last thing any resident wants to do is piss off the clerks. They can make our lives miserable for the duration of our tenure here, and they know it. And they know we know it, too.

As far as I can see, there is nothing else to be done until tomorrow morning. With a little luck, I'll be able to skip breakfast and retrieve the x-ray between morning rounds and surgery.

Up at four-thirty, dressed and on the floor by five, I make my rounds on our twenty-odd patients, ready to report to the attending at six a.m.

"I hear you've lost Mr. Jones' chest film," the surgeon says.

"It never made it over from the clinic, sir."

"Of course it came over. I ordered it to be sent myself. Check at the radiology desk."

"Yes, sir."

No luck at the radiology desk. I make another trip to the clinic. Minutes after seven a.m., the radiology office has just opened. They have no idea where Mr. Jones' x-ray film is, either. "Looks like it was sent up to Six yesterday afternoon."

I run up the stairs to the sixth floor, to the Surgery Clinic, once again. I ask the secretary if she has seen the film.

"Jones? That patient should be at the hospital already. He's supposed to be in surgery this morning."

"Yes, Ma'am. That's why we need the film."

"It was sent over with the patient yesterday."

"Unfortunately, it didn't make the trip."

"You'd better find it!"

"Yes, Ma'am."

Back at the hospital, the patient is waiting in the pre-op corridor, next in line for surgery. I am out of my civvies now, dressed in blue pajamas with matching paper hat, shoe covers and mask in place, walking into the OR to face the consequences of my failed expedition.

"Where's my x-ray, Dr. Stewart?"

"I haven't been able to locate it, sir."

"Why *not?*" he bellows. "Did you see the patient waiting in the hallway?"

"Yes, sir."

"So, the patient is here, ready to undergo surgery. I am here, ready to operate. The anesthesiologist is here, ready to do his job. The nurses are here. Your colleagues are here. And now you're here – *late* – yet we are still unable to begin. Why? *Because we have no chest x-ray.* How am I supposed to operate on this man's chest without knowing what I am looking for? Without the patient's x-ray, I would be operating in the dark. *Blind!* Is *that* how you want me to operate, Dr. Stewart? Is it your intention to put this patient at risk? *Do you want to kill this patient?*"

"No, sir."

"'No, *sir,*' you say. And still I have no x-ray."

"With all due respect, sir, I don't understand how I can be responsible for delivering something that I have never seen – that as far as I can tell never even existed."

The room goes silent. The surgeon turns to face me, his eyes blazing anger. I have forgotten Rule #2.

"*It's your job, Doctor.* Now listen up! We don't need people who make excuses. What we need here are people who care enough about their work and about their patients to get the job *done.* Do you understand that? *Can* you understand that? If you can't do *your job*, we'll find someone else who will!"

Ordinarily threats like this are powerful tools – because fear usually works. Fear is stimulating and motivating, and fear of losing one's livelihood is among the most potent varieties. But somehow, right this minute, losing this job is sounding more and more like the best of all possible alternatives.

I understand the rules of internship. I do. I also understand that they are stupid, and often counterproductive. If busting my ass to fix somebody else's mistake is only going to get my ass busted a second time, I fail to see the payoff - for me, for my patients, for my future as a doctor. I came here to learn how to care for people, not to get chewed out for trying my best to do the impossible.

It seems to me that a better approach to Mr. Jones' dilemma might have been to schedule another x-ray earlier that morning. I would not have been allowed to do that, however, since such a change would have upset the day's carefully balanced operative schedule, and I had no authority to throw such a wrench into the finely-tuned workings of a world-class medical machine. Besides, had I demonstrated the initiative to identify the problem, acknowledge its significance, and fix it pro-actively, I would have missed an essential opportunity for a public dressing-down, and an official affirmation of Rules #1 and #2.

As it happens, Mr. Jones is sent forthwith to get another chest film, and his case is postponed until later in the day. Problem solved, the machine rolls on.

His previous x-ray is never found.

That's probably my fault, too.

Suicide Notes II

"They're killing us here," I said, painfully aware of the futility of my complaint. We were both too tired to die.

It was 1:30 in the morning, and neither of us was anywhere near the end of our respective To-Do lists.

He responded with a wry smile. "Shit, man. We won't let them kill us," he said, looking down at his pager. It was buzzing, again, for the thirtieth time since midnight.

"We can always just kill ourselves, and beat 'em to it." *Maybe the MMPI was right after all*, I thought.

"No, thanks," he said. "We don't have to give them that satisfaction. Not *literally*. Nothing here worth dying for, anyway – only the illusion of a dream that they're using against us. If we make it through this, it will be *our* doing, not anything they did for us. And if we don't, it should be on *our* terms. But kill ourselves? *Hell* no.

"*Social* suicide," he went on, "Now there's another possibility altogether. I say the day we decide we've had enough of this crap, we leave our scrubs and lab coats behind, and head south to the border. Burn our IDs and disappear somewhere deep into the mountains of Mexico. Totally reinvent ourselves. New names, the works. *That* would screw 'em. Just wake up one day and walk outta here. No note. Nothing. Leave the pager on the pillow and go."

Fever

Four-forty in the morning, after a rare night at home. I am stepping out of the shower, about to get dressed before driving in to
begin my morning rounds. My pager goes off, twice in rapid suc-
cession. Dripping wet, I call the nurse's station.

"Mrs. Fabersham is spiking a temp," the nurse says.

"How high?"

"101."

"I'm on my way. Get a urine sample for me, won't you?"

We operated on Mrs. Fabersham the day before. Her temperature
is not particularly high, and not at all unusual for the first post-
operative day. After all, we had just opened up her abdomen like
a suitcase, and spent an hour or more tugging, slicing, snipping,
and stapling her entrails. Her body has every right to be a little
angry.

In this situation, the basic "Three W's" come to mind: *Wound,*
Wind, and *Water.* Seven or eight minutes from now, I plan to look
at the patient's incision for redness (Wound), listen to her lungs to
see if the pain is causing her to take shallow breaths (Wind - this
alone can cause a low grade temp), and check her urine (Water)
for bacteria. Given her relatively healthy preoperative condition,
and the fact that none of these complications is particularly serious at this stage of the game, I am in no great hurry to rush to
her bedside. I finish my ablutions, dress quickly, and head directly
to the hospital.

I arrive at Mrs. Fabersham's room at 5:07 a.m., a full half hour earlier than normal. The nurse at the desk looks worried. "You'd better get in there," she says.

Both the senior and junior residents are already at the patient's bedside, removing the dressing from Mrs. Fabersham's wound.

"Where have you been?" they want to know.

"On my way here."

"Did you know that your patient has a fever?"

"Yes. That's why I'm here now."

"You're *late*. When a patient becomes febrile, you have to learn to respond."

I start to mention the Three W's, and say something about how late I am not. I want to explain that things would have been under control – in fact *were* under control – even before my superiors arrived two minutes ahead of me. Instead, Senior makes a show of writing standard WWW orders: Change dressing three times a day. Encourage breathing. Urinalysis, with a standing order for antibiotics if the result comes back positive.

Out in the hallway, Senior looks sideways at me and says, "You need to get your act together. You should have been here to take care of this - it could have been serious. You were lucky this time."

I was there to take care of this, goddammit.

"Explain something to me," I say. "I'm already up and on my way to the hospital, ready to see my patients. Ready to get here *early* to start to work. I get a call and I respond appropriately. This lady was afebrile at ten o'clock last night when I looked in on her. How was I supposed to know that she was going to spike a fever this morning?"

"It's your job."

I stop dead in my tracks.

"No way," I say. "That's *not* my job."

They stop, stunned, and look back at me.

"Listen. If you tell me to do something, *fine* - I'll do it. *That's* my job. As long as I know *how* to do it, that I am actually *authorized* to do it, and the tools are available that *allow* me to do it, *I'll do it*. Then, if I don't do something right, you can yell at me all you want. *But* – if something happens that I know nothing about, or if I am only told *after the fact* that I was supposed to do something that didn't get done, there's no way you're dumping that crap on me. And I'm sure as hell not going to take any criticism from you for showing up on time, and doing my job well."

My ears are red. By now I'm a little bit febrile, too.

They stand in front of me, wide-eyed and silent.

"I don't read minds, fellas. I don't have a crystal ball, and the Acme Retrospectoscope they forgot to issue me at orientation is broken. So tell me what it is that you need me to do, and let me *do* it. Otherwise, leave me the hell alone."

Senior looks me over for a second longer, then turns away in disgust. Junior leads the way to the next patient on the list.

A moment later he leans toward me and murmurs, sotto voce:

"I've never heard another intern talk the way you do." He betrays a curious, one-sided smile. "You're something else, you know that? They say you don't fit very well in this program."

"Thanks," I say.

"Thanks, nothing. You don't watch out, you're going to get us all in trouble."

He is still smiling, though, just a little.

Lip Service

It was Christmas Eve in the ER. Technically, it was now the *ED*, since there was more than one room involved, and Emergency *Department* looked better on the hospital's administrative chart and promotional literature. (Subsequent confusion between the Department's abbreviated title and the similarly derived term *Erectile Dysfunction* had yet to emerge in the popular culture.)

Since nobody with any seniority would think of working on the night before Christmas, only interns and a couple of exhausted chief residents were left to staff the ER, er, ED, at the World Famous Medical Center.

Enter one condescending middle-aged woman, expensively coiffed, and attired in full seasonal regalia, with a teenager of similar raiment and disposition in tow. The teen was holding a Kleenex to her lip, and appeared to have been crying – the etiology of which (pain, anxiety, embarrassment, ennui) could not be immediately determined.

A careful history, provided exclusively by the mother, revealed that the patient had suffered an accidental nip from Mummy's precious lappy dog (a teacup something derived from one part Pekingese and two parts Poodle – a combination that prompted the ER staff to speculate endlessly on the colloquial variations of "Peek-a-Poo-Poo"), sustained during a round of Christmas kisses with the energetic, but apparently *not* universally affectionate pooch.

Physical exam revealed a potentially pleasant 16 year old Caucasian female in minimal distress, who was persuaded to reveal a 3 mm straight line laceration to the upper lip, perpendicular to and precisely traversing the vermilion border, the anatomical edge

173

of the structure. That singular physical finding, according to the hospital's treatment protocol, meant that a consultation with the Plastic Surgery service was mandatory.

Mother was visibly and vocally relieved by this policy, forbidding that her daughter be ham-handled by some ignorant *general* surgeon, and demanding to speak forthwith to the *plastic* surgeon on call. Since I had rotated onto that service a day or two hence, and since it was after 5 pm on Christmas Eve, I was the "expert" in line to answer the ER's request for consultation.

Six months out of medical school, and still barely able to locate the working end of a pair of forceps, I was arguably the last person who should be given responsibility for anything more complex than copying down an order for Tylenol. The Chief Resident in the ER, just weeks away from finishing his course of training *in plastic surgery*, grinned wryly as he handed me the girl's chart, happy to be relieved of this case's matriarchal burden.

"Hello", I said, entering the exam room (barely suppressing a smile of my own). "I'm the doctor on call for Plastic Surgery. What seems to be the problem?"

The critical problem was repeated to me in a comprehensive maternal recitation of detail and attendant emotion, with emphasis on the necessity of preserving daughter's pristine visage – the very fundament of her hopes for success, personally and professionally – now, and in all the years to come. I smiled and nodded, knowingly.

Fortunately, I was then able to tune Mother out just long enough to anesthetize the scratch, place a single hair-thin suture, and apply a dollop of antibiotic ointment (which matched the girl's fashionable lip gloss, minus the sparkles). I valiantly resisted the urge to sew mother's mouth shut, for good.

"Will there be a scar?" Mother asked.

"Of course," I replied, parroting a physician I overheard once in med school. "My job is simply to make it as small as possible."

"Thank God," Mother sighed, melodramatically. "I knew I was right to demand a specialist!"

"Yes you were, Ma'am. Merry Christmas."

Three Minute Exam

"Don't go in there!" the charge nurse told me. "She's already in a mood today!"

Still learning how to run solo morning jet rounds on a busy surgical service, I had no time today for Mrs. Jones' antics. My job was to see each of my patients (more accurately, visually examine their wounds), check their numbers, write a short SOAP* note to prove I'd been there, then be ready to report on everyone before the Attending appeared at 6:30 a.m. I was ten charts down, twenty to go when the nurses issued their warnings.

Mrs. Jones, a 70+ year-old woman recently widowed, now three days post-op, was uncomfortable. I had not known her to be otherwise. With a list of complaints equal to her impressive assortment of prescriptions, over-the-counter and herbal medications, this patient had earned a reputation for pushing the nursing staff to their limits.

"For God's sake, don't ask her about her stomach," offered one floor nurse. "Or her knees!" added another. "You'll be in there all day!"

For a moment I considered moving on to the next name on my patient list, leaving Mrs. J for last, when hopefully I'd have more time. Little chance of that. I always managed to finish jet rounds just under the wire. There was just no time to backtrack.

On the other hand, I had no time to waste generating explana-

---

*SOAP note: An abbreviated progress note, commenting on the Subjective and Objective aspects of a patient's course of treatment, followed by an Assessment and Plan.

tions for Mrs. Jones' endless somatic complaints, real or imagined. Maybe later in the day, but not now.

No choice but to meet the challenge, I told myself.

I tried to recall the details of a bedside demonstration from medical school, involving a similar patient with a long list of issues. The presentation began in the hallway, before meeting the patient. "Be nice," the professor had told us. "And never relinquish the initiative." Examining a patient is a structured conversation, he said. "Your goal is to come away with meaningful information. Your goal for the patient is for them to feel cared for."

Entering the room with a big smile, I met Mrs. J's anxious expression, her mouth pursed into a tight frown, her eyes lined with concern. "I'm so glad you are here, doctor," she sputtered." You have no idea the trouble I've been through!"

"How's your stomach this morning?" I asked, noting an audible gasp from the other side of the door. I reached for her ankle beneath the bedclothes, checking her pedal pulse.

"Oh, you have no idea! I…"

"Is it as bad as the shoulder trouble you were telling me about yesterday?" I wondered, checking her urine output.

"Why, no, doctor. My shoulder has been giving me fits! It…"

"And how about your bowels? Did that new medicine give you any relief? Once you're up and walking, that problem will take care of itself – and it will help your knees, too. How are they doing today?"

"Well, I…"

"Why, that was a silly question, wasn't it? You've hardly finished your breakfast. Now let's take a look at this incision."

Wound 'A', free of rubor, tumor, calor, or discharge. We chatted for a moment about how well she was doing after her surgery, how her feet were nice and pink, how steady her vital signs were, and how her vigor had improved overall. "Don't worry," I said. "As soon as you're ready, the nurse will be in here to help you get moving. Remember the pain medicine we talked about yesterday will work for your incision *and* for your joints. If you need more, just say so!"

Fresh dressing in place, pertinent numbers lodged safely in my short-term memory, I headed for the door. "I'll check in on you again in an hour or so to see how you're coming along. Good to see you this morning, Mrs. Jones. Have a great day!"

The charge nurse had been standing outside in the hallway, looking at her watch.

"Three minutes," she reported, shaking her head in disbelief. "Three minutes flat."

Commencement

Suicide Notes III

A suicide occurred on or near the campus of the World Famous Medical Center, around the time that my intern class first reported for work. None of us knew the person, since we all had just arrived. 'Another Resident' was all we ever heard.

A different resident suicide, possibly two of them, had occurred the year before. Details were scarce after the WFMC's public relations department took over management of the story. We were advised not to discuss the matter with anyone, under any circumstances.

To hear the PR folks tell it, nothing bad ever happened in these Hallowed Halls of Healing, and nothing ever would, but the story of a doc who nose-dived off of the roof of the hospital (or a hotel, or an apartment building, no one could say for sure) was hard to explain away.

The official account was chillingly statistical: *With X number of people in a given community, a community such as ours, for example, from time to time there would be unfortunate, though* unavoidable *occurrences of this sort. These developments were tragic, of course, and we all mourned the loss of our former colleague(s), who was (were) for some sad and unknown reason unable to function in the challenging and rewarding environment of cutting edge medical training.*

What their rationale neglected to consider was that these numbers were two (or three) times the expected across-the-board average for a 'community' of our size. A community that had not suffered such a loss in recent memory.

A statistical blip, then, we were told, unofficially. *Definitely not a trend.*

But the rumors persisted, as did the questions and the speculation, until one autumn afternoon all surgical residents were called in for a mandatory assembly.

We've heard all the stories, the departmental officials began, *but now it is time to stop dealing in conjecture, and stick to the* facts. *If they happened at all, none of the alleged incidents in question occurred on a surgical service*, we were assured, *and no such event involved a* surgical *resident. So stop worrying about it. Surgeons are tougher than that. Besides, you have too much work in front of you to be distracted by other people's emotional problems. If you don't, we'll give you more.*

(Gosh, I was feeling better already!)

Still, in the unlikely event that any of you find yourselves experiencing misguided thoughts or (ahem) feelings along these lines, we are required to inform you that a suicide hotline has been established for the benefit of all resident staff. A counselor can be reached at any time, twenty-four hours a day, by simply calling the clinic operator. All calls will be completely confidential, and will not be reflected on your academic record.

Now get back to work.

Good to know that any unsanctioned tendencies toward self-destruction I might have had would not be reflected in my permanent record. I instantly felt all of my impending personal crises, if in fact I had had any, which I'd just been assured I hadn't, slip silently away. No worries here. No, sir.

Some time later, after it became clear that I would no longer be harboring any concerns at all about a future in medicine, I did find myself wondering what I would do after my year of surgery was over. Fully engaged in the daily grind of paperwork and patients, I had not yet figured out just how I was going to occupy my time after leaving the hospital. I didn't even have a good idea of where to start. But that day would be coming soon enough, and I needed to start lining up some contingencies.

Surely there were ample resources for addressing this sort of dilemma somewhere within the multiple departments of the WFMC. We were prepared for anything. Said so, right there in the brochure.

Ruminating about alternative career options got me nowhere, though it did finally break me of the nasty habit of studying surgery – which then left me in a quandary about how to occupy the wee hour between midnight and one in the morning, that stepdown period between full-on adrenaline rush, and my usual three or four hours of oft-interrupted slumber. To fill the gap and calm my nerves, I read Thoreau and Heinlein, wrote bits of poetry and snatches of prose, and even managed to draw a few pictures – none of which helped me make any concrete, viable plans for the future.

Could I work in a rural emergency room? Good money in that, I'd heard, but I was barely qualified to be an intern, and that job sounded like an endless extension of residency, with more dead people. No, thank you, please. A book store, maybe? I liked to read, and I sure had learned to keep ample records. But I had no business experience (hardly anyone in medicine did), and that would surely limit my options, wouldn't it? I could try to get an entry-level job somewhere – anywhere, I guess – but I had school loans I would have to start paying back, and minimum wage wouldn't be enough to cover that, plus rent, plus groceries.

Surviving in the real world was never a part of the medical curriculum. I needed professional help.

At some point I started thinking about the academic, psychological and vocational tests that had been administered periodically to all students, from kindergarten to medical school. Annual exams and evaluations ascertained a student's aptitude for science, math, language, music. Problem-solving abilities. Spatial awareness. Eye-hand coordination. College versus trade school, Factory work versus factory design. Hammer versus pencil versus hair gel. There had to be some exam that could tell a disillusioned young surgical intern what his alternative career options might be.

I needed to take that test, and the sooner the better.

Aptitude tests were the purview of the Brain Police, weren't they? I needed, therefore, to talk to a psychiatrist. Not as a patient, but as a colleague – a client, so to speak. That was it. I needed a private consultation.

One problem: I didn't know who to call. I'd been working at the WFMC for half a year, and I had not yet met anyone attached to the Department of Psychiatry. I was a master of clinical paperwork, though. I briefly considered filling out and submitting an official Consult Request, but these, it turned out, were restricted to patients who have been admitted into the hospital, and had an active, clinic-issued patient identification number. Presenting myself to the Psychiatry clinic seemed like a plausible idea, but again, the outpatient services were geared toward seeing actual outpatients, and one had to be referred by another physician to get an appointment.

The solution: call the Suicide Hot Line. Perfect! The Hot Line would provide a direct link to someone on the Psych staff, and bypass all the red tape. One call would make an immediate professional connection, doctor to doctor, and would get my life headed in an entirely new direction in short order.

"Hello, this is Dr. Stewart," I told the operator, trying to sound as calm and sane as possible. "Please patch me through to the Suicide Prevention Line."

"The *what?*"

"The Hot Line. You know, the Suicide Prevention Service."

Nothing.

"We were told back in September that there was a special Suicide Hot Line available for medical residents. I need you to put me through."

"We don't have anything like that here."

"No, seriously. Suicide Prevention. You're supposed to have the number."

"Sorry. They haven't told us anything about it. Let me check the handbook. Hmmm… Nope… Nothing like that is listed here."

"Are you *kidding me*?

"Hey, you're not trying to kill yourself, are you?"

"No, but if I were, I'd sure be one step closer to it by now. Tell you what. Why don't you just connect me with the Psychiatry department, over at the clinic."

"They're closed for the day."

"Thanks, I'll try again tomorrow."

***

"Take a seat, Don."

The Psychiatrist moved out from behind his desk, waving an open hand to two empty chairs facing each other in the opposite corner of his office.

"The clinic secretary gave me your note. It says here that you want to *interrupt* your residency training? Temporarily, I presume. Tell me about that."

"Oh, no, Sir," I clarified. "That decision has been made. I need to find out what I'll be doing after I leave this place."

"That's an unusual course of action, wouldn't you agree?" He said.

"What? Leaving medicine, or trying to formulate a good escape plan?"

"Leaving your residency, of course. That's not a common decision."

"Less common than perhaps it should be," I offered. "There are a number of doctors here who would probably be a lot happier doing something else. Many of their families would be happier, too."

"Is your family upset with you?"

"Not yet, but I have a feeling they are going to be very displeased with me at the end of the year. I'm referring primarily to my parents, of course, though I don't imagine my extended family will be very happy, either."

"Well, something has gotten you upset enough to consider changing the direction of your entire life. Don't you think that's worth talking about?"

"Not particularly. I am not at all satisfied with the state of the art that I've seen during the course of my training. Neither am I happy over the prospect of continuing any farther than I have to."

"Residency is hard on everyone, Don."

"Yes, and I've been told repeatedly it will get better with time and experience. I just have to hang in there. Keep my head down, and keep moving forward. Soldier on through. Do my job, get past the intern stage, and learn what's needed to become a senior resident, then a Chief. After that I will be on my own and can do things the way I want to."

"Exactly."

"The trouble is, Sir, I don't see the point in moving forward. I look ahead and see that the second year residents are just as miserable as the interns. The seniors aren't much better off, and the Chiefs are terrified of their own practices. Once they leave here, novice surgeons either have to scrape together a practice from scratch, or slave away for years before they can buy in to an established group. All along the way, the wives and kids never get to see their husbands, fathers – or these days, some families never see their surgeon wives and mothers. That's five to ten years of loneliness and tension that leads to strained marriages and fractured families. You don't have to look far to see plenty of that kind of damage right here."

"Are you married, Don?"

"No. I'm not. So I won't be letting anyone but myself down by changing directions at this point in my life. But to answer your question, I *have* looked ahead, and frankly I don't see anyone in this business that I want to grow up and be like."

He frowned down at his note pad, rubbing his bushy eyebrows with a thumb and finger.

"Medicine is a *calling*, Don. It's not a gift given lightly. Nor is it a responsibility to be dropped on a whim."

"I understand that," I replied. "Believe me, I understand it very well. By the same argument, though, I cannot in good conscience follow this path if I am not completely dedicated to the profession. And I'm not. Not anymore."

"But the world needs surgeons, Don. There aren't enough to go around, as it is."

"True. The world needs psychiatrists, too. And plumbers, and teachers and bankers and artists. But we need good ones. What we don't need is another bad doctor."

"What makes you think you are a bad doctor?"

"I don't think I am a bad doctor. I just know I'm not necessarily a good one, and I have lost the desire to get better. If I continue along this career path, I am fairly certain that I would *become* a bad doctor."

"So you're lacking in self confidence."

"Possibly. But that's mostly attributable to the fact that I hate my job. The longer I stay, the less I like it. And that's hardly fair to me, or to my patients. The way I see it, leaving the profession now is the most responsible course of action I can take."

"Hmmm...."

"Let me put it to you this way: Would you want someone taking care of your wife or your daughter who *didn't* want to be doing this job? How many of us are already out there, doing that very thing?"

He began scribbling on his pad. "Well. You present us with an interesting problem, Don. Of course I'd like to talk to you more about this. For now," he looked at me and smiled. "We are going to give you a provisional diagnosis of Situational Depression..."

"But I'm not depressed," I interrupted.

"... just something to give us a reason to start a chart on you. Just in case." He continued to scribble.

"Just in case of what? I'm *not* depressed."

"Don't worry, for the time being we will not divulge any of this information to your department. Your medical record will of course be kept confidential."

"Look, I don't care if everybody in the world knows I came here today. I came in with a specific problem, and I'm looking for answers."

"What exactly *are* you looking for, then, Don?" he asked, finally looking up from his notes.

"Career advice. I was hoping you could give me an aptitude test. Something that would help me decide on an alternative career. I need to find something I'll be good at after I leave the scrubs and the stethoscope behind."

"That's an interesting problem," he said, folding his hands in his lap. "One that I'm afraid we won't be able to help you with here."

"Why not?" I wondered. "Isn't that what you people do?"

"Not that I'm aware of. We do administer various tests to our patients from time to time, to determine general parameters of mental health, help with certain diagnoses – but nothing like what you're talking about. It sounds to me like you need a career counselor."

"Bingo. Any idea where I could find one?"

"Actually… no."

Really?

"Then thank you, Doctor. I appreciate your taking time to see me."

"Happy to help. Hopefully we can talk again. And remember, all of this will be kept in the *strictest* confidence."

"Yeah, you said that."

So much for a safety net. I'll be flying on my own from this point forward.

*Secondary Intentions**

I looked up to see her walking toward me down the long, dim
hallway. It had to be at least two a.m., somewhere deep in the
labyrinth, even deeper in the endless Midwest winter season.
From the quiet we might have been the only two awake in the
entire hospital.

She was a beautiful girl, as pretty as she was tired that night, up
working as many hours as I had been, probably more. Her hair
was long and shaded blonde, and combed straight down, surprising since she usually wore it woven in a single braid. Her walk
was different, too, not the sure steps that I recalled. Less business
here, her stride more casual, distracted. Her head was bowed,
shoulders forward, hands thrust deep into the pockets of her
white clinic coat.

I hadn't seen my friend like this before. Hadn't seen her at all, for
that matter, for longer than I could remember. It happens when
you're consigned to different specialties in different parts of a
large hospital complex. Sometimes colleagues don't lay eyes on
one another for weeks at a time.

The distance between us closed steadily. I called out to her, hoping to lift both our spirits for a moment, hoping to shrug off my
own mantle of fatigue, and carry the energy of camaraderie on to
my next assignment.

"Well, look what the cold night wind blew in. Aren't you a welcome sight!"

Her head lifted for a moment, eyes alight. Her lovely face – a face

* Secondary Intention: a surgical term regarding a wound that cannot be
stitched together, but must be allowed to heal from the inside out.

I now realized I had never seen before – bloomed into a warm, inviting smile. From a distance she looked so remarkably like the other, but now, gazing into new eyes, hopeful and lonely as my own, I recognized my embarrassing mistake.

"Oh, I… I'm sorry… " I stammered, feeling suddenly ashamed of myself, and my overtures, so inappropriate, based on mistaken familiarity. "I… thought you were someone else."

Over an instant the light in her eyes flickered, confused, then dimmed to a cool blue sadness. Her hopeful smile quivered and flat-lined, her lovely forehead creased in the familiar pain of rejection, enveloped by an insecurity shared secretly by all doctors in training, doubtless by twenty-somethings everywhere. Her gaze fell back to the floor, and she hurried past without a word.

"I'm Don. What's your name?" I didn't say.

"Excuse me. Do you have time for a cup of coffee?"

"Hey, I've seen you around. Do you have a minute to chat?"

"What have they got you up doing so late at night?"

"Pardon my forwardness, but you reminded me of a friend of mine. I hope that won't prevent us from becoming friends, too."

"Boy, do I feel stupid."

"Hi."

I said none of these things.

I just walked on, feeling tired and dim-witted and shamed, guilty of embarrassing myself and offending this lovely, capable woman.

Primo Non Nocere.

I had ruined a perfect moment, and found myself utterly unable to summon the confidence or the vocabulary to fix it.

I saw her later, once or twice, across the cafeteria or the lecture hall, but we were never close enough again to meet. I never found the chance to speak to her again, though, never engineered another opportunity to introduce myself, to bridge and heal the gap that I had so carelessly opened between us.

For two people on either side of the divide, the wound would have to knit from the inside, in its own time.

Antisocial Behavior

Pale, gaunt, 32 year old white female with facial seams, scars, tattoos and attitude consistent with forty-plus years of rugged life experience, admitted to general surgery floor for treatment of recurrent alcoholic pancreatitis. Patient acknowledged causal connection between drinking and current flare-up of acute abdominal discomfort, which she described graphically, in lurid street vernacular. Clinical impression among surgical staff: TMMBR (Too Many Miles of Bad Road. Pronounced '*Timber*', followed by forearm gesture of a tree crashing to the ground).

NPO* and restricted to bed rest, cut off from her usual choices of social, gustatory and chemical distraction, the patient's attitude declined rapidly. Her mounting discomfort was communicated through anger, defiance, and regular verbal confrontations with medical staff, whose cold, professional demeanor magnified the woman's suspicion of authority figures into outright paranoia.

Per protocol, the patient was placed on an IV drip of morphine, barely sufficient to ameliorate the intense, lancinating pain penetrating her belly, and burning straight through to her back. After two decades of alcohol and opiate abuse, the woman's liver had learned to metabolize painkillers with astonishing efficiency.

The nurses increased the dose to the maximum allowable limit, with little added benefit. Unable to achieve adequate relief, the patient continued to communicate her displeasure with increasing frequency, volume, and venom, eventually alienating all three shifts of nursing staff.

Nil per os – Nothing by mouth

"Give me something that fucking *works!*" she spat at anyone who came within earshot, her voice torn with anger, tinged now with fear and desperation.

No one did, since no one could. Soon no one would want to.

"That woman in 312 is driving us crazy, Doctor," one of the floor nurses told me. "Go in there and see if you can do something about it."

Two days in to a new, six-week general surgery rotation, I was anything but this woman's doctor. The attending physician's name was on the chart, and there were two residents and a clinical fellow above me who were making the decisions regarding her care. I was there to see that their orders were carried out, to keep the paperwork up to date, and to be on hand to respond to emergencies until the real docs arrived.

That day I was alone. The surgeon and senior residents were away, seeing patients across town in the clinic. I was left to face the wrath of the patient, the nurse – or worse, *both* – entirely on my own. I steeled myself for the meeting.

"How are you feeling?" I asked, mustering my best effort at a warm smile.

"You know goddamn well how I'm *feeling*," she spat, clutching her abdomen for the effort. "I feel like *shit*, that's how I feel. I hurt like hell all the time. When are you and those other white-coated SOB's gonna *do* something about it?"

"Well. Let's talk about that. You know why you're hurting, right?"

"'Cause I'm a *drunk*. That's what the nurses say, anyway."

"It's because of your drinking, that's true. We're not sure why, but your pancreas doesn't like it when you drink. It gets angry and swollen…"

"You're telling me! *I'm* the one doing the goddamned hurting."

"What else do you know about your pancreas?"

"I ain't no doctor. How am I supposed to know anything about it?"

"Well, the pancreas pumps out juice that digests your food. When it swells up this way, it starts digesting *you.*"

"Then why don't you fix it? All you bastards have done so far is make me your goddamned *prisoner!* You won't let me eat or drink *anything!*"

"Unfortunately, that's what it takes to help you. We have to let your digestive system rest before it can heal. That's what we're trying to do…"

"But it hurts, *dammit!* It hurts *bad!*"

"We're giving you all the pain medicine we can…"

"*I don't believe you,*" she hissed, squeezing back tears. "If there was morphine in that bottle, I wouldn't be hurting this much!"

"*Listen,*" I shot back, quietly but firmly. You've got the liver of Superman. It chews up drugs faster than we can safely pump them into you. Besides that, pancreatitis is serious pain. You're going to be hurting, even with large doses of medicine."

She continued to glare at me, but I could tell she was listening.

Finally.

"Now we both know you're a tough lady. You'd have to be, or you wouldn't have survived a lot of the stuff you've had to deal with in your life."

Her gaze shifted from side to side, finally settling on the twisted corner of bed sheet she was clutching between her fists. "I still think the goddamn nurses are lying to me," she said. "They're not giving me as much dope as they're supposed to."

"What if I could prove it to you that they are?

"How're you gonna do that?"

"Do you know what naloxone is?"

"You mean *Narcan*?" she said, calling the drug by its proprietary name.

"That's right. Naloxone counteracts the effects of morphine, but only for a little while. It doesn't last long."

"So what?"

"I want to give you a tiny dose of it. Just a whisper, okay? If the nurses are giving you the medicine they're supposed to, you should feel the pain increase almost immediately. It will only last a minute or two, but that should be plenty of time to decide whether or not we are really trying to help you. I'll only do it with your permission. Will you trust me?"

After a long moment, she looked up again, and slowly nodded her head.

***

Within seconds of injecting less than half a milligram of the drug into the patient's IV drip, the lines in her face began to draw together. Her jaw tightened. Too stoic now to cry, she squeezed my hand until the pain subsided, and the relative calming effect of the morphine returned.

"Take another slow, deep breath," I told her. "Are you okay?"

"Yeah. It's better now."

"I know it doesn't always seem like we're being friendly around here, but everyone in this unit is working hard to make you better. Do you believe me?"

"I guess so. It just hurts, that's all."

"I know it does. But being afraid of the pain only makes it worse, and makes it last longer. You have control over your own fear, and I'll bet there's not much in the world that can scare you. So you need to hang in there, and trust us to do our job. Can you do that?"

That night my patient slept soundly for the first time since her admission.

She continued on a steady course the next morning. Everyone thought it was funny that she ignored the senior resident's instructions, and kept referring to me as 'her doctor'. The Attending refused to even see her, insisting that his resident staff handle this case from beginning to end. "That woman's crazy," he said.

No surprise, then, to find her room empty on afternoon rounds.

"They sent her to the Psych ward about an hour ago," the woman's nurse told me.

My patient had been 'turfed' to Psychiatry – dispatched to the care of another medical specialist – not so much for her own good, but to get her out of our hair.

The paperwork had been filed earlier in the day. No one saw any need to apprise the intern of the transfer. The senior resident would follow the case from a distance as a surgical consultant. I would never have the chance to see the woman again.

"Something about her needing a behavioral assessment, and addiction management," the nurse continued, distracted. "Good riddance, if you ask me."

Taking the Blame

People make mistakes. Interns, usually. Nurses, too. Patients.
Residents, of course – less so as they survive each stage of the
program, and climb the academic pyramid to seniority, security,
and eventual infallibility. For those of us who haven't yet made
it that far, well, we still have a tendency to screw up. And, hopefully, own up.

Already scrubbed in for an hour or better on the search for a
fugitive, hyperactive parathyroid gland, a procedure challenging enough without repeated interruptions, all present (save the
patient, who was asleep) were repeatedly distracted by the appearance and reappearance of the OR charge nurse, who had been
combing the halls outside for our next patient, the one already
overdue in the operating room next door.

It wasn't her fault, she said, and said again, and kept saying. The
nurse claimed to have no idea why Patient X had not yet arrived
in the OR suite. She was ready to do her job as soon as he appeared. Until that happened, his absence was not her responsibility, even though she acted very much like it was. Every few
minutes she would return to update the surgeon, to let him know
that no progress whatsoever had been made in locating the missing patient.

With each interruption, the surgeon grew ever more irritated.
(That wasn't her fault, either. She was, after all, doing everything
she could do.)

Oddly enough, neither was it the intern's fault. Not this time, anyway. My paperwork apparently had been in order on this patient,
my instructions clear. According to the unit clerk upstairs, our
man had been shipped down from his room over an hour ago.

He should have been stationed in the pre-op waiting area, ready to go.

So no one was calling me to task on this one. Not yet. Knowing that the scenario was prone to change at any moment, however, I decided not to bask in any false delusions, choosing instead to focus intently on the operation, and do my best not to call attention to myself – which included suppressing the urge to suggest that perhaps our patient might have turned himself in to a radiograph, and vaporized in transit.

It may be correctly presumed that the boss, our surgeon, had a schedule to keep, and that schedule required Patient X (whose name easily could have been Ray, come to think of it) to be present, prepped and ready for the next operation on the day's list. His other team of residents was already on hand, and prepared to scrub in. The disappearance of Mr. X threatened to upset the entire morning line-up.

"But I don't *know* where he is", the nurse said, popping in once more to declare her innocence. "Someone just isn't doing their job!"

Clinging tenuously to his last professional nerve, the surgeon looked up from his work and spoke to her in a calm, stern voice. "At the moment, madam, it appears *that someone* might be *you*."

"But I'm telling you it's *not my fault!*" she cried, now on the verge of an all-out tantrum, her words echoing shrilly around the room.

No one knew what could happen next. Confrontations such as this between nursing staff and surgeons were virtually unheard of. The room grew silent, the atmosphere tense.

"It was *my* fault," said the scrub nurse, flatly, breaking the silence. The lean young man in his mid-twenties usually kept to himself, as he had been this morning, quietly assisting the surgeon throughout the procedure.

"I did it," he repeated.

This was an absurd statement, as everyone present knew. The day's operating schedule required this man to be in the room - this *very* operating room - scrubbed and gowned and watching over his instrument trays uninterrupted since five o'clock that morning. He could not possibly know anything of Patient X, except that other people had been arguing over the unknown patient's unknown whereabouts for nearly an hour.

Tuning in to the spirit of camaraderie that often permeates a well-functioning OR (a phenomenon that in some rooms borders on telepathy), the surgeon picked up on his assistant's cue. "*Your* fault, you say?"

"Yes, sir," the young man replied. "My fault."

Everyone could feel the tension begin to melt away.

"Well at least that's finally established. Now that we know whose fault it is, maybe somebody else can get about finding our missing patient. *You*, young man, are obviously not qualified."

"No, sir," agreed the assistant.

The charge nurse, now absent the protection of her excuse, left the room in tears, in every bit of a huff.

It was the first time I could recall ever seeing anyone voluntarily accept blame, let alone assume culpability for something they plainly had not done. This young man stepped up and took one for the team, and it worked. Brilliantly.

Suddenly, all the energy that had been expended in a fruitless mis-direction of responsibility was refocused on actually solving the problem. In a matter of minutes the patient was located, identi-fied, and wheeled directly into the adjacent room.

This was a lesson I would remember for the all that was left of my time as an intern, and afterward, for the rest of my life: *Blame anyone, but get on with the job.*

Our truant Patient X had actually been present all along, lying just outside of our operating room, tucked into a corner of the hall-way behind a drawn curtain – sound asleep. Absent the hearing aids I had asked him to leave with his wife before the operation, he was totally unaware that the nurse had been calling his name, over and over again.

Auditory solitude, working in silent concert with the drowsy pills I had prescribed for him the night before, rendered the man bliss-fully oblivious of the turmoil I had caused.

Oh, yes, the blame for this one could be traced directly back to the actions of the intern.

It was my fault.

Entirely.

Bubbles

This is my last day at the World Famous Medical Center.

Tomorrow the new crop of interns will arrive on campus, wide-eyed and eager to serve. Seasoned interns will become junior residents. Juniors will become seniors, seniors will be chiefs. Chief residents today will start new fellowships, or head out into the world to begin practicing on their own.

Tomorrow I will be pulling a U-Haul trailer to a tiny river town, to reinvent myself as a writer, an artist, a shoe salesman – anything but a physician-in-training.

A duck-row of doctors files down the hall of the Urology floor, world-renowned urological surgeon Dr. Zeigler at the head of the line. He is followed in order by the Chief, then the senior and junior residents. I am the feathers on the tail end.

Dr. Z leads us into a dark and empty patient room. He flips on a recessed light box, slides a sheet of plastic film from a wide envelope, and pops it into the clips on the wall.

"This is your test, " he says, addressing us all. "We shall see what you have learned on this rotation." Pointing to his Chief, he continues, "Doctor. Your diagnosis?"

At first we all think that this is a joke. Eyes still adjusting to the dark, we find ourselves squinting and staring at a full-sized radiograph, mottled gray from edge to edge. There are few, if any, discernable landmarks. No tissue edges, no white patches of bone or injected dye, no dark air pockets – just one unbroken mass of hoary fluff.

We have nothing. No answers. Not even any clues.

The Chief clears his throat. "Is this some kind of trick question? It looks like an X-ray of a pillow."

"Not at all," says Dr. Z, pointing to the next in line, the senior, who will be his new Chief tomorrow. "You."

"Adipose tissue? Is this patient obese?"

"No."

One by one, the others try their hand at deciphering the cloudy, enigmatic plate. No one has the slightest idea what we are seeing. I am no exception. I do have a small advantage, though. Being the last in line, I have more time to study the problem, and I know more about what the image is not.

I also have the least to lose, so I'm willing to take bigger risks.

While the others stammer, stutter, and shrug, I look at the dull gray image and let my imagination run free. When Dr. Z. calls my name, a few of the pieces have started to fall into place.

"What do *you* think, Dr. Stewart, who are so soon to be leaving us for a life of leisure and creativity?"

"I see circles," I say, feeling my way through my own thoughts. "More truthfully, I have convinced myself that there may be vague circular densities present throughout the radiograph, kind of like piles of soap bubbles filled with smoke… which doesn't make much sense until you consider the physical dimensions of the X-ray film. These are *big*. The size of the plate indicates either a thoracic or abdominal exposure. Nothing else is wide enough. And the fact that there are no bone densities present rules out the chest."

Hearing no rebuttal, I decide to continue. "The absence of bone also tells me that this is not an A/P or P/A shot, a full thickness, front-to-back x-ray, since either would clearly show a white spinal shadow. If this is in fact a radiograph of a human subject, it must be an abdominal tomogram, with the X-ray camera focused on a thin, horizontal slice of abdominal soft tissue. From a *big* abdomen.

"But that doesn't account for the absence of air in the field. There are no black spots. There should be abdominal gas present, unless the bowels are being pushed out of the way, displaced by a mass of some sort."

My hypothesis seems to be holding together, so I continue: "So we are left with an abdominal mass that looks like smoky soap bubbles, which would suggest a cystic process in the kidney or liver...

"With that in mind, I'm looking closer to see if there are any other distinguishing features, and I imagine I can see faint dividing lines between what appear to be three different regions of grey foam. The only thing I know of that can account for all of these findings would be polycystic disease involving both kidneys and the liver."

There is a long moment of silence.

Okay, so I'm wrong, I decide. It was a good story, and I'm outta here anyway. They can't do a thing to me, other than reiterate how stupid I am. I'm home free.

Dr. Z shakes his head. "After today," he says, "One of you will be starting his own practice. Two of you will be advancing one year, and one step closer toward your own careers as urological surgeons. None of you were able to make this diagnosis. The only one among you who arrived at the correct answer was the *artist!*"

He turns back to me. "Dr. Stewart. You are an excellent diagnostician. This proves you must remain in medicine."

"Not really, Sir. It only proves I'm good with black and white pictures."

Dr. Ziegler opens the door and leaves the room, duck line in tow. I lag behind for a moment, rearranging the gear in my jacket pockets: stethoscope, peppermints, patient notes, drawing pad.

"Our next patient is *this* way, Dr. Stewart," Dr. Z says impatiently. "Won't you be coming with us?"

"No thank you, Sir," I say, heading toward the elevator.

"You are *not* dismissed," he says, a familiar authoritative edge in his voice. "Our rounds are not yet finished."

I glance at my watch. 5:01 pm.

"I'm sorry, Doctor," I smile, handing him my pager. "But you'll have to continue without me. As of now I am no longer employed at this institution."

Shrugging out of my jacket, I bypass the open elevator doors, loosen my tie, and take a deep breath before launching myself down the stairs toward the ground level, taking the steps three at a time, surgeon-style.

I emerge from the hospital into a bright, sunny summer afternoon, feeling like I have just been liberated from a lifetime sentence of hard labor. Without question, this is the healthiest move I will ever make.

.

Past Medical History

Appendix

Numbers

The year is 1985.

You are a 1st year surgical resident at a large academic medical institution.
How much is your time worth? Let's do the numbers…

There are 24 hours in a day.
There are 7 days in a week.

$$7 \text{ X } 24 = 168$$

There are 168 hours in a week.

Subtract 4 hours per night for sleep (a generous assumption)..

$$4 \text{ x } 7 = 28$$

$$168 - 28 = 140$$

You work 140 hours per week.

Subtract 90 minutes (1½ hours) per day for meals.

$$1.5 \text{ X } 7 = 10.5$$

$$140 - 10.5 = 129.5$$

On second thought, add them back, since every minute you spend in the hospital is on the clock. Regardless of whether you are finished with your meal, have just started to eat, or are standing in the cafeteria line waiting to be fed, the job requires you to set your tray aside and answer your pager whenever it beeps.

The same priority applies to your other bodily functions.

So, we're back to 140 hours per week, or 280 hours every two weeks.

Actually, since you are on a 24-hour call schedule, add your 28-hour sleep time back again.

140 + 28 = 168

So, you work 168 hours a week, or 336 hours every two weeks.

168 X 2 = 336

You are allowed to be off duty for ½ of a day, every other week, for R&R, laundry, housework, car repairs, and family time. Subtract 12 hours every other week for time off.

336 – 12 = 324

No, make that 10 hours every two weeks, because sometimes there is too much work to do to let you off for an entire Sunday afternoon.

336 – 10 = 326

That's 326 hours every two weeks, or 163 hrs/wk you spend on the job.

Your job requires you to work 163 hours per week.

You are allowed 2 weeks for vacation every year – unless the hospital needs you to work during your selected vacation period.

Let's assume that you get your vacation anyway.

52 – 2 = 50 working weeks per year.

Since a residency is a salaried position, there is no consideration for overtime. This makes your hourly rate of pay an easy number to calculate:

163 hours per week X 50 weeks = 8150 hours per year.

You are paid somewhere in the neighborhood of $20,000.00 per year (again, a generous assumption). $20,000 divided by 8150 = $2.45.

You are earning $2.45 per hour.

The federal minimum wage in 1985 was $3.35 per hour.

2.45 divided by 3.35 = 0.73, or 73%

You are earning less than 3/4 of minimum wage.

Since a residency is a salaried position, this is legal.

By comparison, in 1985 the average plumber's "helper" (apprentice plumber), earned approximately $16,500.00 per year, working a standard 40 hour week, 50 weeks per year[1].

40 X 50 = 2000 hours.

$16,500 divided by 2000 hours = $8.25 per hour.

2.45 divided by 8.25 = 0.296, or 30%

You are earning less than 1/3 of what an apprentice plumber makes.

As an intern, you are the front line of patient care. You are the doctor that the patient sees every day. You are the professional who receives all laboratory and test information pertaining to your patients. You are the one that the nursing staff calls when problems arise.

How much is your patient care time worth?

On a busy hospital surgical service, you may see 30 patients per day. On a light hospital service you may see 5 patients per day. (There are few light hospital services.) On a clinical service, you may see 20 patients or more per day. On any service, you may be called to see 5 additional consult patients per day.

Let's assume, conservatively, that you will carry an average of 15 patients per day.

$15 \times 7 = 105$

You will make at least 105 individual patient visits per week.

$105 \times 50 = 5,250$

You will have 5,250 patient interactions per year.

You are paid $20,000.00 per year.

20,000 divided by $5,250 = 3.81$

Your individual patient care visits are worth $3.81, however since you round on your hospital patients at least 2 times per day, **your actual care time is worth closer to $1.90 per patient visit.**

Forget the plumber. That's closer to waitress pay.

And you're not even allowed to take tips.

Should Have Been A Plumber

Back in 1985, you're eighteen years old, and just about to graduate from high school. What will you be? Plumber or Doctor? You're smart, energetic, and a quick learner. Everyone tells you to be a doctor, of course. But what do the numbers say?

Plumber Pay

In 1985 an average apprentice plumber could earn approximately $8.25 per hour. That's $16,500.00 a year, right out of high school. No waiting, no college debt, and you even get health insurance and a retirement plan.

After two to six years (let's say you're motivated, and shave it down to four), you finish your apprenticeship. You are now qualified to hire out your services as a journeyman plumber. Your hourly wage increases to $12 an hour, and continues to increase with experience and a little luck to $16. After ten years you're up to $24.

Gross income for your first fifteen years out of high school is around $435,000.00, give or take. Your average income is nearly thirty thousand dollars per year. Not all that much, but you're able to lead a pretty good life for a single guy. You are still debt free, and already have a good start on your retirement. At 33 years old, things are just going to get better.

By 2010, your average annual plumbers' salary is around $50,000, with tenth and 90th percentiles at 27K and 79K. Your income is expected to increase by more than 10% by 2018.[2] If your credit is good, you can get an affordable loan (and an exceptionally good deal) on a $150,000 house.

On the down side, you've had to work hard, expose yourself to germs and job-related injuries, and are required to spend the big holidays away from home.

You are however making lots of money, living well, and improving peoples' lives, keeping them comfortable and free of disease.

You're still smart, energetic, and a quick learner. Assuming you have made some valuable connections in the industry, there is every reason to believe that you will work closely with your colleagues to learn the business side of plumbing, and may even leverage some of your savings and sweat equity to start your own business. (Better yet, you may leverage some of your savings, sweat equity, and your growing relationship with the boss's daughter to buy into an established family business.) Either way, you are now in a much better position to capitalize on your experience, and build a brighter, more profitable future.

Even without any engaging in any entrepreneurial ventures, by 2018 you can expect to gross an additional $900,000.00, earning your first million by the time you're fifty. There is every reason to expect that with your continued hard work, experience and connections, your income will rise through the $75 - 100K levels, and with inflation may easily reach $150K by the time you are in your sixties. If you choose to retire at 65, you will have made well over $5.3 Million.

But You Wanted To Be A Surgeon

In 1985, general surgeons earned an average of $175,000.[3] Academic surgeons earned considerably less, with much of the difference offset by the absence of rising malpractice and health insurance premiums, continuing education opportunities, paid support staff (including resident physicians) and retirement benefits.

But none of this means anything to you, except the salary. It's BIG. You just graduated from high school, and have decided you want to be a doctor.

First, you have to go to college. Let's pretend your parents aren't in the plumbing business, and aren't going to be able to pay for this dream. You'll borrow the money to pay for tuition, plus books and living expenses – and that's okay. You're going to be a doctor, and doctors make lots of money.

According to the Congressional Budget Office[4], the average tuition for a year of training at a qualified undergraduate institution was $2300.00. Ignoring inflation, you'll pay that amount for four years. (For the sake of consistency, we'll also ignore living costs, assuming they are close to those of a plumber's apprentice.) By the time you earn your degree, you're $9200.00 in the hole.

That's okay, though, because you were accepted into medical school! Congratulations! You will be expected to attend lectures and laboratories for four to eight hours a day, not counting study time – which will consume most of your evenings and weekends. Your overall debt from this experience will be somewhere between $22,000.00 and $27,000.00[5]. We'll make it an even $24K, or six thousand per year. At least you are covered by the university's health insurance plan.

Once you graduate, you're just over $33,000.00 in debt. (While you have been studying, your plumbing counterpart has made more than a hundred and sixty thousand dollars, spends plenty of time with his friends and family, and gets to go fishing every weekend.)

Fortunately, you landed a choice spot in a fine surgical residency program, where you will be getting a salary for the first time, and at $24K, it's better than apprentice pay – only he's now making $28K as a journeyman. Your salary will increase by $2000 each year, except for that one year of laboratory research – which you hope will help you look better when you apply for a specialty fellowship position six years from now. Yes, you still have health insurance, but no retirement benefits yet, other than Social Security. The hospital will also pay for your state medical license and your malpractice insurance as long as you're working there.

On the down side, you work very hard (likely over 100 hours per week – your plumber friend works 40, plus a little overtime, for which he gets paid extra), expose yourself to germs and job-related injuries, and are required to spend the big holidays away from home. Eventually, though, you will be making lots of money, and improving peoples' lives.

By the time you finish your extended surgical residency, you will have earned $135,000.00 over 14 years (note that is *less* than ten thousand a year), if we pretend that you paid off all your loans before they started accruing any interest. Chances are you did not (since $10K a year is not much to live on), in which case you are still carrying a significant and growing debt load. Meanwhile, your pipe-wielding counterpart has made $300K more than you. And he gets to go home at the end of every day.

Your training continues for another three years during your specialty fellowship in Thoracic and Vascular surgery, during which time you will still work round the clock, but you will be paid a little better.

Unfortunately for you, the ACGME regulations limiting resident workload to 80 hours a week will not be instituted until the year after you have completed your training. The change would have mattered little, however, since any work not done by residents under the new schedule would simply have been shifted to you, the salaried fellow.

Hopefully your marriage, if you have chosen that route of emotional and practical support (residents have precious little time to wash their clothes or keep house), is still intact. The odds are stacked against it (one surgery program actually boasted a 96% divorce rate to their applicants[6]), however in the interest of pleasantry and easy math, we will assume that you are not paying anything in the way of alimony or child support. Your salary has entered the 40K range, and will rise to 50K before you are through.

You have earned another $135,000.00. The plumber has earned another $144,000.00.

Now is your chance to catch up with your labor-intensive cohort. As a board-certified thoracic and vascular surgeon, you may expect to start making $125,000 per year in private practice, once you have completed your training. If you find the right location and the right practice model, you may earn up to $350,000.00 per annum by the end of your career. Again for simplicity's sake, we will assume the best for you, along with a regular rise in compensation throughout the course of your practice.

It will take you another four years before you finally catch up with the plumber, simply counting your respective gross incomes – a full twenty years since you both graduated from high school. The fact that he has had more time and resources to invest in a home, a business, and a retirement plan with compounding interest drives the catch-up date even further ahead. The costs involved in setting up your own clinic, or buying into an existing practice will likewise extend the point of parity into your future, as will the added burdens of malpractice insurance, clinic staff, membership in professional associations, and continuing education. Large purchases such as a home, auto, beach condo, etc. may keep the clock ticking well into your mutual retirement.

Conclusion?

If you want to make money, be a plumber.

References

[1] http://www.ssa.gov/oact/NOTES/note135.html
[2] U.S. Department of Labor
[3] G C Pope and J E Schneider, Trends in Physician Income *Health Affairs* Vol. 11, no.1 (1992):181-193
[4] Maureen A. McLaughlin *TRENDS IN COLLEGE TUITION AND STU-DENT AID SINCE 1970*, Congressional Budget Office, Dec 1988
[5] Paul Jolly, Ph.D., *Medical School Tuition and Young Physician Indebtedness*, Association of American Medical Colleges March 23, 2004
[6] Donald Stewart, M.D., Personal conversation, 1985

Past Medical History

Year	Plumber	Doctor
1986	$16.5 K	($2.3K)
1987	16.5	(2.3)
1988	16.5	(2.3)
1989	16.5	(2.3)
1990	24	(6)
1991	24	(6)
1992	26	(6)
1993	28	(6)
1994	30	24
1995	32	26
1996	34	28
1997	36	28
1998	40	30
1999	44	32
2000	48	40
2001	48	45
2002	48	50
2003	48	125
2004	48	130
2005	48	135
2006	48	140
2007	49	145
2008	49	150
2009	**49**	**155***
2010	50	160
2011	50	165
2012	50	170
2013	50	185
2014	51	190
2015	52	195
2016	53	200
2017	54	225
2018	55	235
2019	60	245

Year	Plumber	Doctor
2020	65	250
2021	70	255
2022	75	260
2023	80	265
2024	85	270
2025	90	275
2026	95	280
2027	**100**	**285****
2028	110	290
2029	120	295
2030	130	300
2031	140	325
2032	150K	350K
Totals:	$ 5,375K	$ 6922K

* Break-even point, when the doctor matches the plumber's gross income:
Age 42, after 24 years of work.

** After expenses, when the doctor finally catches up with the plumber:
Age 60, after 42 years of work.

Past Medical History

Acknowledgments

Past Medical History

A thoughtful review of the 50 years since I and my brother were obliged to "sit still and be good" (neither of which we did very well, or for very long) in doctors' offices and hospital waiting rooms reveals a lengthy cast of characters: parents, grandparents, step-parents, teachers, coaches, counselors, professors, hospital and clinic staff, friends, classmates, colleagues, art directors, editors and mentors who, while sadly unable to realize any significant improvement in my behavior, have been instrumental in the development of this collection of stories, and without whose energies and interest this book could not have been possible.

Among the first contributors to the successful production of *Past Medical History* were Darlene Barr MD, Nancy Blake, Alan Blum MD, Elaine Owen Chambless, Frank Franklin MD, Robben Leaf, Rufus Partlow MD, Dane Petersen, Norman Rose PhD, Mark Schumacher MD, Marty Sharkey MD, Mary Sue Stranathan, Michael Teixido MD, and Rev. Daniel Vickery, whose comments and feedback shaped the final version of the book.

The publication of *Past Medical History* was accomplished largely through the convenience of the crowdfunding organization Indiegogo (www.Indiegogo.com), and the overwhelming generosity of friends and supporters of the DS Art Studio, who have kept us in groceries for a very long time, and who responded enthusiastically to our call for support. My sincere thanks to Madelyne Absher, Katy Anderson, Vicki Anderson, Wanda Argersinger, Saji Azerf, Richard Banks, Wade Black, Betsy Blake Berrier, Ree Bolton, Leah Boozer, Cheryl & Mark Bourn, Larry Bowen, Jim and Beverly Brock, J.R. Brown Jr., Suzan Buckner, Nancy Burleson, Marc & Becky Butler, David & Katie Buys, Kathleen Rose Byington, Phil & Ilene Candreva, Kay Canupp, Joe Carley MD, Mark & Amy Catledge, Karen Catlett, Mary Jane Coker, Mathew & Amanda Crawford, Margaret Lyn Cushman, Rick, Gina, & Annabella Sophia D'Andrea, Annette Dennis, William DeVan, Alan Dimick MD, Barbara Pinklady Eddins, Mike Evans & Zebrah Savage, Jaydie Gamble Fay, Judy Finch, Rolando Flores, Lindsey

Fitzharris PhD, Betsy Frazer, Ouida Fritschi, Darryl Fuhrman, Cathleen Garcia, Charles Ghigna (Pa Goose), Ginger Gidden-Weinzierl, Sandy Giroux, Jean Greenwood, Sharon Griffitts MD, Barry Guillot, Mary Deyerle Hack, Roy Hager MD, Leanne Harper, Cass Hayes, Jack Heidt, John & Tanya Hendrix, Daphne Holcomb, John Hosmer, Jim Howell, Mike Howell PhD, P. Reginald Hug DC, Connie and Mike Hulsey, Eddie Hyatt, Charles & Gwenn Jackson, Ron & Jill Lovik, Kristina Kauss, Gene Lammers MD, Alethea Lewis, C.S. Lewis, MSgt Tom Lewis, Sabrina Lewis, Karen Loach, Duane Pontius & Naomi Logsdon, Joni Lohr, Rozalyn Love, Valerie MacEwan, Pam Maget, Dr. Tom & Twinkle Martin, Kelly Masters, Margaret McCain, Debbie McDonald, Billie McElwrath DC, Terry McKay, Norman McSwain MD, Branko Medenica, Heidi Medenica, Dr. Greg and Judy Merijanian, Aaron Merijanian,Alexis Merijanian, Capt Joe Moore USN Ret, Kay Moore, Nancy Moore, Sarah Morgan MD, Mark & Barbara Mullins, Mark Mullens MD, Patty Newgard, Andy & Dee Nickens, Sharon Norton, Revs. Jim & Dorothy O'Quinn, Katie & Dean Page, Randy Page, Anne Palmer, Rebecca Pardo, Julie Parker, Debbie Patton, Will & Mary Piens, Ray & Lisa Pietz, Deborah Pinnick, Leah Pyra, John Quattlebaum, Tina Quave, Catherine Rains, Marlene & Tony Ralston, Barbara Reinhart, Rick & Susan Remy, Libbie Rodgers, Marlene & Tony Ralston, Kathleen Rose-Byington, Antoinette Ross, Susan Ross, Bob Rosser, LtCol Norm Root USMC Ret, Nancy Lowe Ruggles, Melinda Sapp, Katie Sasser, Lee Saylors, Mary Ann Scheppler, Lisa Schoff, Mark Schumacher MD, Tom & Barb Shaper, Kenny Rex Shuler, Col. Clarence A. "Butch" Shelton III USAR Ret, Wayne Shew PhD, Michael & Minay Sirois, Sally & Steve Smith, Mary Sowell, Fern Spackman, Madeleine Sparks, Hank Spencer, Dave & Sharon Stewart, David K. Stewart, John F.P.B. Stewart, Lynn Stranathan, Martha Summey, Ken Takeda, Imogene Tilson, Ricky Tilton, Scott Trites, Brittany Uno, Hahn Vu, Betty Vaughn MD, She She Vaughn, Katherine Walcott, M. Wells, Jeff and Marie Welna, Thomas C. White, Neal Whitt, Martha Willetts, Wendy Williams, James Woodard MD, Lee Yarberry, Dr. Chris & Erin Yuskaitis.

Special thanks to David Hill, whose critique of these pages made them inestimably better, and on whose suggestion they came together in a single volume; to Cristopher T. Chandler and *Stegosaurus*, for their musical inspiration; and to Sue Ellen Brown, who has been listening to these stories for years, and has hardly complained about it at all.

The author also wishes to thank the editors of the following journals, who were kind enough to allow an experimental writer the opportunity to see his work in print, and encouraged him repeatedly to make amend(ment)s:

Past Medical History
Originally published in Pulse magazine, January 2011,
Paul Gross & Diane Guernsey, Eds. www.pulsemagazine.org

Bob War
Published in The Dead Mule School of Southern Literature,
October 2013, Valerie MacEwan, Ed. www.deadmule.com

First Grade, First Day
Originally published in the Birmingham Arts Journal,
Jim Reed, Ed. Volume 4, Issue 3, 2007

A Familiar Face
Originally published in Southern Humorists, August 2009,
Sheila Moss, Ed. www.southernhumorists.com

Treating the Numbers
Originally published in Pulse magazine, December 2010,
Paul Gross & Diane Guernsey, Eds. www.pulsemagazine.org

Lip Service
Originally published in Southern Humorists, April 2011,
Sheila Moss, Ed. www.southernhumorists.com

Section Illustrations

Introduction: *Cancer*

Pre-Pre Med: *Toy Horse*

Pre-Med: *Left Brain, Right Brain*

Med School: *Clown Doc*

Graduation: *Trombones*

Internship: *Quack*

Commencement: *Hummingbird*

Sketch Pad

Past Medical History

Progress Notes

Don Stewart

Sketch Pad

Progress Notes

Don Stewart

Sketch Pad

Progress Notes

Don Stewart

Sketch Pad

Past Medical History

Progress Notes

About the Author

Don Stewart managed to earn a doctorate in Medicine, after finagling an undergraduate degree in both Biology & Art by indulging in drawing, painting and design as a change of pace from his premedical studies. He continued to dabble in art through medical school, and despite the persistent distractions of a surgical internship, he succeeded in creating his first commercial composite drawings, and won awards for short fiction and poetry – all in a valiant, though some would say not entirely successful effort to hold on to the fringes of sanity.

In the end Dr. Stewart chose to leave his medical studies behind, and focus his energies full time on more creative endeavors. In compliance with the prime medical directive (*Do No Harm*), he never actually put his medical license to use, working instead as an artist, writer, and creative consultant at the DS Art Studio, where he eventually attained the position of Chief Visual Humorist.

Continuing to focus primarily on his signature style of drawing, he currently limits his medical practice to endorphin management, and obscure disorders of the funny bone.

Don's short stories have appeared in *The Dead Mule School of Southern Literature*, the *Journal of Irreproducible Results*, the *Placebo Journal*, *Pulse* magazine, *Southern Humorists* and the *Birmingham Arts Journal*, among others. His artwork can be seen online at

www.DSArt.com